MYSTERIES IN OUR NATIONAL PARKS

MYSTERY
#6

Birthday
Book Club Donation
by

Megan
Harvey

10-20-96

Mary E. Silveira School

MYSTERIES
IN OUR NATIONAL PARKS

GHOST HORSES

GLORIA SKURZYNSKI AND ALANE FERGUSON

NATIONAL GEOGRAPHIC SOCIETY
WASHINGTON, D.C.

Maps by Carl Mehler, Director of Maps;
Thomas L. Gray, Gregory Ugiansky, and Martin S. Walz,
Map Research and Production
Running horse art by Stuart Armstrong

The legend on pages 55–57 is adapted from "Wild Thing," as
published in the *BLM National Horse and Burro News,*
Spring 1999.

This is a work of fiction. Any resemblance to living
persons or events other than descriptions of natural
phenomena is purely coincidental.

Library of Congress Cataloging-in-Publication Data
Skurzynski, Gloria
Ghost Horses / Gloria Skurzynski and Alane Ferguson
p.   cm. — (National parks mystery ; #6)
Summary: Visiting Zion National Park with his family, twelve-year-old
Jack encounters two mysteries, the strange behavior of a band of wild
mustangs and the possibly sinister actions of his new foster brother, a
Shoshone boy.
ISBN 0-7922-7055-X (Hardcover)
ISBN 0-7922-7667-1 (Paperback)
[1. Wild horses—Fiction. 2. Horses—Fiction. 3. Zion National Park
(Utah)—Fiction. 4. Utah—Fiction. 5. Shoshone Indians—Fiction.
6. Indians of North America—Fiction. 7. Foster home care—Fiction.
8. National parks and reserves—Fiction. 9. Mystery and detective stories.]
I. Ferguson, Alane. II. Title. III. Series.
PZ7.S6287 Gh 2000
[Fic]—dc21   00-027730

Printed in the United States of America

ACKNOWLEDGMENTS

The authors want to thank Denny Davies,
Chief Naturalist, Zion National Park;
Donald A. Falvey, Superintendent, Zion National
Park; Tom Haraden, Assistant Chief Naturalist,
Zion National Park; and Gus Warr, Wild Horse
and Burro Specialist at the Cedar City Field Office,
Bureau of Land Management.

Our very special thanks go to our patient
friend and fellow writer Lyman Hafen, Executive
Director of the Zion Natural History Association,
and to Art Tait, Cedar City Field Office Manager,
Bureau of Land Management, who introduced us
to Mariah and who spent so many hours driving
us across the Chloride rangeland to educate
us about wild mustangs.

For Kristin and Matt
We wish you a lifetime of happiness.

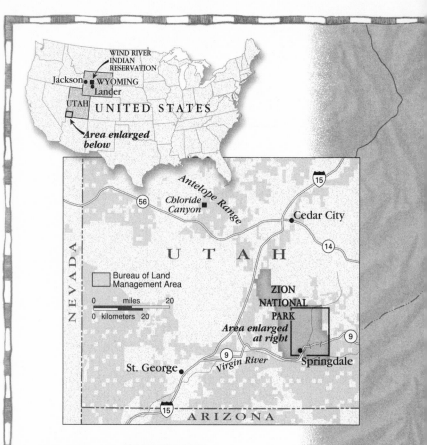

PARK DATA

STATE: Utah

ESTABLISHED: 1919

AREA: 146,551 acres

NAME: Huge rock formations reminded Mormon pioneers of the temples of God, so they named the canyon after the heavenly city.

NATURAL FEATURES: Massive sandstone cliffs, deep, narrow canyons carved by the Virgin River and its tributaries, and spring-fed hanging gardens that cling to canyon walls

Towers of the Virgin

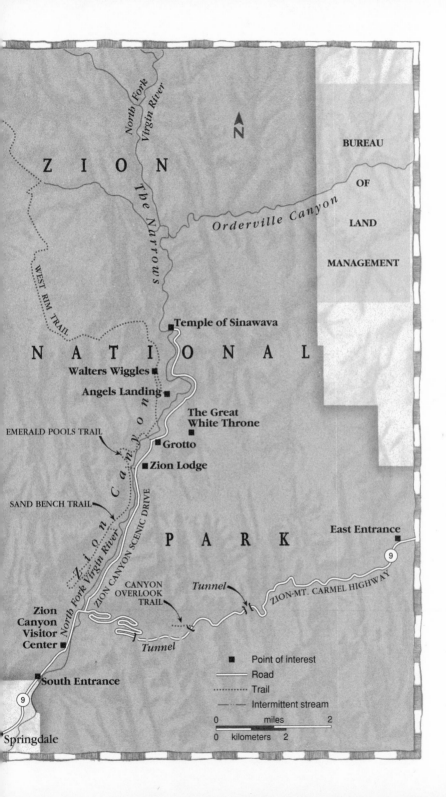

A rough branch drilled into his chest, like a skeleton's finger, but the man knew he couldn't change his position. Even the smallest flicker of movement would let them know he was there, and the man had spent too much time setting the trap to tip them off now. Behind him he heard the rustling of flanks against juniper trees. He held his breath when he saw it—a flash of silvery white, so pale it seemed as if a piece of moon had dropped from the desert sky. A Ghost Horse.

As he watched it move closer to his trap, the man tried not to think of the strange stories he'd heard, tales of white horses that whinnied a language of their own, caught between this world and the next. The mustang, ghostly white, stepped inside the trap. The man leaped out of the blind and slammed the gate shut. He had his prize.

Again and again the mustang hurled itself against

the rails, rearing up before slamming into them in an explosion of sound. It gave a strange, ghostly cry that echoed back from the hills. Then he heard the pounding of hoofs. Frightened, the man turned and ran.

CHAPTER ONE

War cries cut the air in quick, high-pitched bursts until Jack's ears rang with the sound. In front of him, 200 Native Americans from dozens of tribes danced through the arena, some with spears in their hands, others clutching eagle feathers as they swirled and pulsated in a dizzying, rainbow-hued parade. Jack had never before been to a powwow. He wished he could go out there and dance to the pounding of the drums instead of just sitting with his sister, Ashley, on hard bleachers.

"Isn't this great, Jack?" Ashley enthused.

"Yeah. Great." He meant it. It just wasn't cool to sound as gushy as his sister.

There was so much motion and color that Jack had to keep switching his gaze, from the gate where more and more dancers swept in, to the far side of the grounds, where horses pawed and snorted, held in check by wildly dressed warriors. The Indian riders looked strong and fierce, with their faces painted and their headdresses bristling with feathers that made them seem larger than life. One carried a yellow shield decorated with buffalo images and red feathers. Another, wearing a black vest and beaded armbands, swung a war club above his head; yet another raised a spear as he galloped his horse in tight circles. How would it feel, Jack wondered, to be a part of something that had been passed down from one generation to another, so far back that no one could remember where it began? To know about your ancestors—unlike Jack, who didn't even know the name of his own grandfather.

"Can you see Ethan or Summer?" Ashley asked, straining to catch a glimpse of the Landons' new foster children in the crowd of dancers.

"Right over there. On the other side of the circle, by the sign that says Eastern Shoshone Indian Days."

Shading her eyes, his sister strained to see. With her own dark hair braided into long ropes and her end-of-summer tan, Ashley could have fit right in with the rest of the dancers. Jack, whose hair was blond and straight like his father's, felt a little bit out of place, since there were almost no other Anglos sitting close by.

"I still don't see them," Ashley pressed. "Where are they?"

"Ethan's next to the chief with the humongous

headdress. Summer's in the middle of the circle next to the lady in the buckskin. See where Dad's standing underneath the sign taking pictures?" Jack pointed. "They just went past him."

"Oh, yeah," Ashley nodded. "There they are. Wow, Ethan's dancing like crazy. Look at him go!"

Dressed in a bright blue vest and chaps edged with an eight-inch fringe, Ethan Ingawanup whirled in circles so fast that the fringe stood straight out from his body. A wheel of feathers three-quarters as tall as Ethan was attached to his back, like a fanned-out peacock's tail. His feet moved as though they had a life of their own, furiously beating against the dirt so that it churned up in tiny puffs. Twenty-three different tribes were taking part in the Shoshone Indian Days celebration, all dressed in ceremonial regalia. Each footfall of the dancers hit the ground like a hammer blow timed to the beat of the drums. One dancer, half his face painted in a white mask, spun in front of Jack. The bronze skin of his naked torso rippled with muscle as he moved close to the earth before reaching for the sky, up and down, like a bird soaring and diving through the air.

Summer, Ethan's younger sister, danced in the inner circle. Her dress was encrusted with silvery, cone-shaped jingle bells that made a tinkling sound as she moved in tiny, mincing steps.

"I'd like to dance like that," Ashley said. "But I'd rather do the dance Ethan is doing, because Summer's hardly moving. Wouldn't you like to learn that warrior dance?"

"Maybe. Yeah, I guess."

"Do you think Ethan would teach us?"

"I doubt it," Jack muttered.

Ashley's dark eyebrows edged up her forehead as she asked, "What's your problem, Jack? You're acting like you don't like Ethan."

Jack just shrugged. He didn't want to get into it with his sister, even though he knew her well enough to figure she wouldn't drop the subject. He took a swig of Coke from his can and tried to get back into the spell of the dancing, until he felt a tug on his arm.

"You ought to try, you know. Liking him, I mean." Ashley moved closer to Jack on the bleacher, so that the toe of her tennis shoe pushed against his. "There's lots we could do together with them, especially since Ethan's your age and Summer's mine, instead of the other way around. It's perfect."

Coolly, Jack studied his ten-year-old sister. He'd always found it a bit hard to deal with the foster kids who spun in and out of their lives like shoppers flung out of a revolving door. "Emergency care" kids, that's what they were called—children who needed sheltering for a short time. Ashley enjoyed them more than Jack did, but he'd managed to make it work somehow. He'd pretty much decided he could get along with any-one, until that morning when they'd picked up the two newest foster kids from Indian Child Welfare. They were different.

Summer, a ten-year-old Shoshone girl, had been as quiet as a ghost, watching their every move with a sad moon face that never changed expression. If they were only supposed to take care of Summer, Jack wouldn't have worried. It was her brother, Ethan, 12 going on 13, Jack didn't know what to make of. From the moment they'd met, Jack had noticed the anger flashing behind Ethan's dark eyes, the way he'd stared at Jack as if he were the enemy. Even though they'd been together only a couple of hours, it was enough for Jack to make his own conclusion: Ethan was going to be trouble.

"Look—if you want Ethan to teach you to dance, then ask him yourself," Jack said, taking a fierce bite of his Indian fry bread. "I plan to stay out of his way."

Ashley crossed her thin arms over her Indian Days T-shirt. "Oh, great, Jack. go on, act like a toad."

"Hey, Ethan's the one, not me."

"At least he's got a reason," Ashley said, boring her eyes into his. "How'd you like it if you were Summer or Ethan?" Inside, Jack groaned as Ashley held up her hand and ticked points off on her fingertips. "First"—her index finger went up—"their parents die in a car crash. Then"—her middle finger shot into the air—"the grandmother who raised them gets put in a nursing home. Now"—Ashley finished with her ring finger—"they've got to leave their reservation and go off with strangers—you and me, Mom and Dad—who they never even met before today."

"I know all that," Jack snapped. "I'm just saying there's something really weird about that Ethan."

"Like what?"

"Like, I don't know—lots of things. When we were waiting in the lobby at Social Services, I gave him a piece of gum. You know what he did with it?"

Ashley shook her head, causing her braids to bounce against her back like black ropes.

"He threw it in the garbage. He didn't chew it, didn't even open it—he just dumped it. Then he looked right at me, like he was daring me or something."

"Maybe he doesn't like gum."

"That's not it." Jack raised his voice to be heard over the beat of a nearby drum. "He's got some kind of attitude, you know? And the worst part is that we're stuck taking them to Zion National Park with us tomorrow. They could ruin our trip, which really ticks me off. Especially since Dad and I are going on a great photo shoot in The Narrows, just him and me. There's no way I'm gonna let that get ruined. I wish we'd never gotten Ethan."

"That's dumb. How could he ruin your trip?"

"Who knows? Anything can get screwed up when you're dealing with a punk like him."

"The key to Ethan and Summer," a voice from behind them broke in, "is time. You just need to give them time." When Jack whirled around, he saw Vivian

Swallow, the social worker who had placed Ethan and Summer in the Landons' care.

Jack could feel the heat rush to his cheeks. Caught! Caught mouthing off. If Vivian Swallow told Jack's mother and dad what he'd just said, he'd be in real, heavy-duty, industrial-size, no-way-out trouble. "I…I didn't…," he stammered.

"It's OK, Jack," Vivian said, placing a hand on his shoulder. Right away Jack knew this woman wouldn't tell. She was as warm and forgiving as Ethan was cold and hostile.

Half Shoshone, Vivian had high cheekbones, wide-set eyes flecked with green, and hair streaked with honey-colored strands. She'd dressed up for the pow-wow in an elkhide sheath beaded with brilliant Indian patterns. Two long fur pelts were attached to the ends of her braids; they hung down below her knees. Leather moccasins made her footsteps so soft that Jack hadn't heard her coming up next to them.

"I see your dad over there, but where's your mother?" Vivian asked.

"She's standing in line waiting for the food," Ashley answered.

Vivian turned to Jack. "I'm sorry. I didn't mean to eavesdrop, but I couldn't help overhearing what you said about the Ingawanup kids. Is it OK if I sit here with you two?"

"Sure, I guess," Jack told her, scooting away from

Ashley to make room. His cheeks still felt hot from embarrassment.

Vivian turned to Jack, her large eyes resting on his. "So you're not real happy about Ethan. No, it's OK." She stopped Jack as he began to apologize.

"Jack thinks Ethan's mean. Is he?" Ashley asked.

Vivian smiled, revealing perfect white teeth. "I like how you get right to the point, Ashley. Maybe Ethan might be, well, just a little less than friendly. Let me explain." Flipping the long fur braid decorations behind her back, Vivian looked from Jack to Ashley, then back to Jack. "Here on the Wind River Reservation, most people watch out for their own. Families take care of families. But unfortunately, right now there's no one who can offer a home to Ethan and Summer. Which means I had to place them outside the reservation. Those two are leaving the only life they've ever known, and that's tough."

"What about their sister?" Ashley asked. "Mom said there was a big sister who's going to be their guardian."

"That's right, but Tamara won't be back for five more weeks. She wants to finish out her college semester before returning to Wind River."

Ashley pressed, "You still didn't say why he doesn't like us."

"Well, it could be because there's been...um... trouble between Ethan and some of the town boys outside our reservation."

"You mean Ethan fought with the white kids?"

Vivian nodded and patted Ashley on the knee. "You're a smart one, aren't you?"

"So Ethan thinks we're like them, right? Like the kids who fought him."

"Maybe." Vivian nodded again, this time more slowly.

Jack leaned forward so that he could see Vivian's face better. "But, I don't get it. If Ethan doesn't like Anglos, then why did you put him with us? I mean, isn't that the worst thing you could do?"

"Two reasons. First of all, right now there's no one else. I was going to try to pull a lot of strings to keep them at Wind River, but then I hit on the second reason."

"What's that?" Jack asked.

"Well, I figured putting Ethan with kids—good kids like you and your sister—might help him more than anything else."

The music stopped and the dancers began to scatter, like bright leaves in the wind. Vivian looked off into the distance. Her voice softened as she added, "Ethan needs to see people as people. Maybe we all do." Straightening, she said, "Well, looks like the food line's starting to move. Let's get over there with your mother. Has either one of you ever tasted buffalo before?"

"Never," Jack answered as Ashley cried, "No way!

Is that what they're giving us to eat? Buffalo? Yuck!"

"Really, it's great!" A tiny smile bent the corners of Vivian's mouth. "Looks like Ethan and Summer aren't the only two who'll be experiencing something new!"

CHAPTER TWO

When they left the powwow, the sun was still high above the horizon, a pale yellow disk against a flat, washed-out sky. As Jack looked through their car window, the reservation land appeared bleached. All around him, small buildings the color of sand blended into grassless hills that disappeared into nothing. After all the color of the dances, the area beyond the powwow seemed to have dried up and faded.

"Aren't you going the wrong way, Dad?" Jack asked when he realized his father had left the main highway and was now heading north on a dusty ribbon of road.

"We can make it from Wind River to Jackson Hole in"—his father, Steven, glanced at his watch—"two hours, which means we can stop at Sacagawea's grave and still get home with plenty of time to pack for our big trip to Zion." Looking at Ethan's reflection in the rearview mirror, he said, "You have an advantage on us, Ethan, since your suitcase is already loaded up. We Landons still have to get our act together."

Silence.

"So, have you ever been on an airplane?"

Ethan pressed his forehead into the glass and said nothing. His long hair covered his face like a waterfall, shutting them out.

"How about you, Summer?" Steven asked, ignoring Ethan's silence.

Summer just shook her head no.

Great, Jack told himself. He could see it now—an entire vacation filled with his parents fussing over Ethan and Summer while the two of them sat like stone. Sighing, he read a road sign, a small rectangle that looked as unassuming as a tag at a rummage sale. It pointed to the cemetery. A moment later they pulled into the tiny parking strip.

As Jack got out of their Jeep, he thought how Vivian Swallow had been both right and wrong. She'd been right about the feast: The roast buffalo tasted wonderful. It was a lean, tender meat without a gamey flavor. Even Ashley liked it. Of course, she'd also piled her plate high with sweet corn and ripe watermelon and beans and salad and a dessert that looked like a cherry cobbler. The feast had definitely been worth staying for.

But Vivian had been dead wrong about Ethan. He hadn't said a word—not during the feast, not when they'd said good-bye to Vivian, not when Jack's mother, Olivia, told him how happy she was to be taking the Ingawanup kids to Zion, not even when Jack's father, Steven, tried to draw him out by telling him about the years he'd spent as a foster child himself. No matter what the Landons tried, nothing worked. Ethan answered everything with a stony silence, as if the only thing that would make him and his sister happy would be to have the Landons disappear.

Now Steven and Olivia hung back beside the Jeep, their heads close together as they spoke in low voices—talking about Ethan and Summer, Jack figured. His father kept rubbing the back of his neck with his hand, a sure sign that he was worried.

Jack felt awkward just standing there at the cemetery entrance, so he finally called out, "Come on, Mom and Dad, what are you waiting for? Let's go."

"Why don't you kids go on ahead?" his mother answered. "Your father and I need to talk for a minute." Wisps of dark, curly hair escaped from underneath a baseball cap Olivia had pulled low on her forehead. She often wore T-shirts with pictures of animals on them. Today, she had on a green shirt with the footprints of different extinct species scattered across it.

"Go on, son," Steven told Jack. "Ask Ethan and Summer to show you the Sacagawea monument. We'll join you in a bit."

Great, just great, Jack fumed. Well, the faster he

went, the faster he could get this whole thing over with. "Summer, do you know where the grave is?"

She looked up at him, her dark eyes wide. Jeez, she can't even answer a simple question, Jack thought.

"I'll take you." Spinning on the tips of his running shoes, Ethan led the way. Now that Ethan was out of his dancing regalia and in a white T-shirt and jeans, Jack could tell how compact yet strong he really was. His arms moved loosely at his sides as he hurried up the hill, so fast Jack and Ashley had to scramble to keep up. As he moved, shoulder-length black hair flew off his face, revealing a strong jaw set in a hard line. Although Summer looked delicate in her yellow-flowered sundress, she had enough energy to follow her brother with no apparent problem.

"Slow down," Ashley called out, but Ethan kept moving at top speed up the narrow path. Determined not to let them beat him, Jack began to jog up the incline, leaving his sister to tag behind. Gravestones dotted the wild grass like scattered teeth, some of them tipped to one side, others with the surface worn to a smooth polish, the letters rubbed bare. Many of the markers were simple slabs of wood. Although some seemed neglected, most of the graves were adorned with bright plastic flowers in every color of the rainbow, as though someone had scattered a giant bag of candy across the barren ground. It was a wind-blown, dusty place. Hardly what he expected to see as the final resting place of someone as famous as Sacagawea.

Ethan and Summer had stopped in front of the largest tombstone. More plastic flowers adorned the grave, along with nickels, dimes, and quarters that had been pressed into the baked earth. The coins caught the sunlight and threw it back like tiny mirrors.

Casting a wide shadow, the large rectangle of granite showed the probable dates of Sacagawea's birth and death, along with a bronze plaque that detailed her life.

"Thanks for waiting, Jack," Ashley panted when she joined him.

"Sorry."

"It's OK. Wow, here it is. I've heard so much about her, how she was the guide for the Lewis and Clark expedition even though she was really young. I can't believe I'm standing right at Sacagawea's grave." Ashley took a breath and added, "She was a Shoshone too, right?"

"Yes. But she's not buried here," Summer answered in a small voice. "Sacagawea died in the mountains. No one knows where her body lies. They made this to honor her."

Ashley shot Jack a triumphant look that seemed to say, "See, she talks!" Placing her hand on Summer's arm, Ashley said eagerly, "I think Sacagawea was a real hero."

"To you," Ethan said sharply. "Not to me. Not to my sister."

Jack and Ashley looked at Ethan in surprise. "Why don't you think she was great?" Ashley asked.

Ethan's thick brows knit together. "She helped the white man, and the white man took all our land. My grandmother said Sacagawea should not have helped anyone but her own people."

Nodding, Ashley tried to get him to keep talking. "I bet your grandmother taught you a lot of things, didn't she?"

"Yes. She taught us the old ways," Summer answered for him. "She taught us the traditional way to dress. She taught us how to cook and hunt and even how to dance, like we did today."

Ashley beamed, triumphant over the fact that Ethan and Summer Ingawanup were finally opening up. "Do you think sometime, maybe later, you could teach Jack and me how to dance like that? I'd really like to learn."

Ethan snickered loudly. His eyes rolled to the sky as he muttered, "I'm not teaching no white guys."

That did it. Jack felt irritation surge through him. "Look, Ethan, whether you like it or not, the four of us are stuck together. Do you think it would kill you to stop being a jerk for a couple of weeks?"

"Jack—don't—" Ashley began, but Jack didn't care. He moved right in front of Ethan, staring him down, eye to eye. "You know, we didn't ask for you to stay with us, but you're here with our family. So why don't you give up the attitude, OK? Then maybe we can get through this until your big sister comes back, and then you can go home and forget about us white people."

Ethan stood with his legs spread apart, his arms crossed over his chest, his eyes hard. Wind began to blow over the hill, bending the grass toward the ground like stalks of wheat, moving Summer's hair in dark wisps across her face. Jack wasn't about to back down, and neither, it seemed, was Ethan. Finally, like clouds parting, Ethan's face cleared. With what looked almost like a smile, he said, "OK."

Nothing Ethan could have said would have taken Jack more by surprise. "OK...what?" he asked, still not believing Ethan's turnaround.

"OK, I'll try to be friends." Smiling slyly, he said, "So you want to learn how to dance?"

"Sure," Ashley answered, nodding eagerly.

"Then I'll teach you. I'll teach you and your brother the Ghost Dance."

Summer pushed the hair off her face, saying, "No, Ethan—"

"Yes. It's a good dance, very old. Gotta be danced around a cedar tree." Ethan looked completely different when he smiled. His teeth were white and square in his dark face, but the smile didn't make it all the way up to his eyes—they still glittered coldly. "Don't worry," he told them. "You'll like the Ghost Dance." Without another word Ethan spun around and began running through the gravestones, higher and higher in the cemetery grounds until he veered off at the top of the hill. Summer followed him, glancing nervously over her shoulder as she went.

"I guess we're supposed to follow them," Ashley said.

"Except there's no way I'm going to dance. Not here. Not with Ethan."

Ashley's voice rose half an octave. "What do you mean? We can't tell Ethan 'no' when he's finally trying to be nice. You've got to."

"You dance. I'll watch."

"No way!" Grabbing the edge of his sleeve, Ashley tugged hard. "Please!" she begged. "Maybe it'll make us all friends! Besides, at the powwow you said you wished you could dance like them."

"That's not the same thing. They had costumes and drums. Out here I feel stupid!"

"No one will see! Besides, our whole trip to Zion will be ruined if we don't get along with them."

That much was true. He looked around the cemetery. His parents, still talking, were finally making their way up to Sacagawea's marker, but beyond them the grounds were completely empty. Jack heaved a sigh. "OK. But if any stranger shows up, I quit. And let go of my sleeve. You're stretching my shirt."

As he and Ashley climbed toward the Ingawanups, Jack noticed that Ethan seemed to be searching for something. After a few minutes Ethan began kicking rocks away from the ground around a small green tree that stood no more than two feet high.

"Hey, watch where you're kicking those things," Jack yelled. "One of them nearly hit my sister."

Summer murmured, "Ethan, maybe we shouldn't do the Ghost Dance...."

Her brother ignored her. "I just needed to clear some space around this cedar tree. I told you that's what we're supposed to dance around—a cedar tree." Impatiently, he gestured for Jack and Ashley to come closer. "Go ahead," he told Summer, who asked him, "You sure, Ethan?"

When Ethan nodded, Summer said in her soft voice, "Stand around the tree. Boy, girl, boy, girl. Take hands." Jack grasped Summer's hand as if in a handshake, but she shook her head and said, "No, like this," and twined thin fingers through his.

Since there were only four of them, the circle was small—Summer, Jack, Ashley, Ethan. His voice low, Ethan began to sing:

> I'yehe' Uhi'yeye'heye'
> I'yehe' ha'dawu'hana' Eye'de'yuhe'yu!
> Ni'athu'-a-u' a'haka'nith'ii
> Ahe'yuhe'yu!

Tugging Jack's hand, Summer moved in a circle from right to left, left foot first, followed by the right one, barely lifting her feet above the ground as they moved. Awkwardly, Jack stumbled along; on his other side, Ashley had caught the motion perfectly and danced as though she'd always done it that way. Ethan's voice grew louder, pounding each note like a beat on a tom-tom. Jack guessed he was singing the same song over and over, although the words sounded so strange that Jack could not tell whether they were being repeated or not.

He glanced down the hill to the Sacagawea monument, where his mother and father stood looking up at the kids and smiling, probably thinking how sweet it was that the four of them were doing a little circle dance together. Probably figuring that everything was all right now. But was it?

His attention was jerked back to the dance, because Ethan had stopped his chant and Summer began to speak. Her voice soft, her eyes half shut, she murmured, "Grandmother's grandmother saw the big fire on the mountaintop. Our people were dancing the Ghost Dance. They danced. They danced. The fire burned higher." Summer spoke in a monotone, her voice neither rising nor falling, but for some reason it made Jack's scalp prickle.

"Grandmother's grandmother saw the smoke. It rolled down the mountain. It covered the earth and the people and the animals. No one could see, but they kept dancing. The smoke got thicker. It hid the sky. It hid the earth. It hid the horses, and turned them into ghosts."

Now Summer spoke in a singsong. "After two days

the smoke was gone. After two days the horses were gone. They became ghost horses. But sometimes, when the people danced, the ghost horses returned."

While she told the tale, Summer's eyelids drooped lower and lower, while Ashley's eyes widened until the whites showed. As for Jack, he caught the smell of—no, that was crazy. He couldn't be smelling smoke—there wasn't a wisp of it showing anywhere, nothing rising into the perfect blue sky, and from that high on the hill he could see all around. Then Ethan began to sing once more, louder than before,

I'yehe' Uhi'yeye'heye'
I'yehe' ha'dawu'hana' Eye'de'yuhe'yu!
Ni'athu'-a-u' a'haka'nith'ii
Ahe'yuhe'yu!

By that time, Steven and Olivia had climbed closer to where the kids danced around the little cedar tree. They were still 20 feet away when Ethan stopped abruptly and pulled his hands away from Ashley's and Summer's.

"Oh, don't stop," Olivia begged. "That was charming."

Ethan became stone man again. He didn't say a word.

"I loved it!" Ashley exclaimed. "Can we do it again? Maybe when we get to Zion National Park? Ethan says we need a cedar tree; I bet there's lots of cedars in Zion. You'll do it again, too, won't you, Jack?"

Jack didn't know whether he wanted to dance the Ghost Dance again. It made him feel off balance, and not just because of the strange rhythmic words that he couldn't understand. It was something more, something he couldn't quite wrap his thoughts around.

But the dance could be a way to keep things smooth between himself and Ethan, and for that reason alone he should agree to do it once more. What did it matter, anyway, if he shuffled around in a circle while Ethan sang, or chanted, or whatever you called it—Jack didn't know whether the words had any meaning at all.

That part about the horses, though, that Summer told—that part was different. Ghost horses. Ghost horses moving across the empty plains in search of—what? He shivered a little, even though the mid-September sun felt warm on his arms.

"Won't you, Jack?" Ashley's voice broke into his thoughts.

"Sure, I'll dance again," Jack replied softly. He wasn't agreeing to make Ashley happy, or to connect with Ethan and Summer or to make the trip to Zion run more smoothly. He would dance to see if in a different setting, under a different sky miles and miles from here, he would still smell that hint of invisible cedar smoke.

CHAPTER THREE

Here we are, riding in an SUV made in Korea, Jack thought. Look at us: two Shoshone kids; my mom, whose four grandparents came from Italy; my dad, with a Norwegian mother and a father who could have been from anywhere, whoever he was—my dad never knew him—and us, Ashley and me. I guess this mixed-up carload is about as American as you can get.

"Hey, what are you thinking about?" Ashley asked him.

"Nothing. Just where things came from." Stretching his arms, Jack asked, "Hey, Ashley, do you know what they first named this park, before they changed it to Zion?"

"I don't know," Ashley shrugged. "What?"

"It was Mukuntuweap National Monument, in 1909. It didn't get named 'Zion' until 1919."

Wrinkling her nose, she said, "Mukuntuweap? Did I say it right? What a weird name."

"It's Indian," Ethan told her. He pulled his eyes away from the window long enough to say, "This used to be Paiute land. They hunted here. This land was taken from them, just like Yellowstone was taken from us. But their spirits are still here."

"Oh," Ashley answered, shifting uncomfortably in her seat. "Well, anyway, it sure is pretty around here, no matter what the name is." Ethan grunted and looked out his window, pressing his forehead into the glass.

They'd rented the sport utility vehicle at the airport in St. George, Utah. Now, as they approached Zion, the flat, sandy earth changed into spires of red rock that brushed the sky like enormous statues. Eons of upheaval and erosion had molded the Navajo sandstone into strange rock formations, here rounded from wind and rain, there transformed into snaggletoothed summits that seemed to bite the clouds. As they neared the park, red rock monoliths rose up into the sky, so tall that even when he craned his neck, Jack couldn't see their tops.

"OK, stay on this road until we come to Zion Lodge, which is right in the canyon," Olivia told Steven as she peered at the map. "The park has booked us into three connecting rooms. Isn't that great? We get to stay in the same building where I'm giving my lecture!"

"I never knew marrying a wildlife veterinarian would buy me a ticket into so many wonderful places," Steven told her. "I just hope you won't be giving your talk in a room with a big window. I mean, who would want to listen to a speech on animal pinkeye when there's this kind of beauty all around?"

"Excuse me?" Olivia cocked her head toward her husband. "Are you saying that you don't find my topic fascinating?"

"Hmmm. Pinkeye in the deer population. I couldn't sleep all last night just thinking about it." Steven, who had a large, lopsided grin on his face, stole a quick glance at Olivia.

"Steven Landon, you know my lecture isn't on pinkeye—pinkeye is just one example I'm using to show how the different branches of the government handle their animal problems. For instance, Zion won't treat the pinkeye in their deer, since it's national park policy not to interfere with a naturally occurring disease. The Bureau of Land Management, on the other hand, treats pinkeye with antibiotics...."

"My mom is a wildlife veterinarian," Ashley whispered to Summer, who was sitting beside her in the very back of the SUV. "She helps rangers if there's a problem about park animals. Lots of times we get to go with her to national parks all over the country. We've seen wolves and manatees and grizzlies and cougars and all kinds of stuff. It's really cool."

Summer nodded quietly, her eyes wide. "Are they fighting?"

Ashley answered, "Fighting? You mean my mom and dad? No!"

Jack turned in his seat to explain, "Dad just likes to give Mom a hard time. They tease each other, you know?"

Summer looked puzzled.

"...so it's very important to grasp the different approaches." Olivia bit the side of her lip and said, "Tell me the truth, Steven, is it boring?"

Steven answered, "Nah. I promise, it's riveting!"

"I don't know why you have to be such a brat," Olivia told him, punching his arm.

"Just doin' my job, ma'am," Steven replied with a laugh.

Funny, Jack thought. He knew his parents well enough to tell when they were kidding, but Summer and Ethan didn't seem to grasp that kind of banter. Had their grandmother ever joked with them? Had she taken them out to ball games or to movies or to do any of the thousand things Jack took for granted? What was their life like on the Wind River Reservation? He was about to ask them when his mother exclaimed, "Look at these canyon walls! The map says they're just 2,000 feet from here to the tops, but they look much higher."

"Yeah," Steven told them, "and this skinny little Virgin River we're driving along sliced right through that solid rock to make the canyon. Like a hot knife through butter. Only it was not just water, but the particles of rock in the water that kind of scoured it out. Did you know a million tons of sand and rock get swept out of this canyon every year? And it only took a couple hundred thousand years for all this to happen."

"How about the next couple hundred thousand years?" Ashley called out. "What'll happen to it then?"

"Don't know. You check it out when you get there and send me a postcard, OK?" Steven joked.

"Ha ha, very funny, Dad. Like I'll still be here in the year 200,000!"

"Give or take a few centuries," he quipped. "What about you, Ethan? Summer? What are your plans for the year 200,000?"

Summer and Ethan didn't even smile. They just stared at the sheer walls of rust-colored sandstone that rose like skyscrapers on both sides of the road. It was as though the Landons were speaking a language the Ingawanup kids didn't understand.

As they swung around a bend, Steven slowed to a stop. A barricade blocked the road that led to the lodge; beside it, a park ranger in uniform was holding up his hand in a "halt" signal.

"What's happening?" Ashley asked.

"We'll find out, as soon as I can figure out how to open this window." Steven fumbled with the unfamiliar buttons on the inside of his door until he hit the one that controlled the windows. All four windows rolled down at the same time.

The ranger, so tall that he had to bend forward to reach eye level with Steven, said, "You'll have to turn back, sir."

"What's the problem?" Steven questioned.

"A horse got loose up there." The ranger gestured toward the lodge.

Olivia leaned over to ask, "You mean one of the horses from a guided tour group?"

"No, ma'am, this is a wild mustang, and I do mean wild. It's been kicking up a storm. We're afraid someone might get hurt if they get in the way of the capture, so we've asked the lodge guests to stay inside till the horse gets caught. Also, we're trying to keep vehicles out of the parking lot."

"How on earth did a wild mustang get into Zion?" Olivia asked. "There aren't any wild herds anywhere near the park, are there?"

"No ma'am. But this horse broke out of a trailer, and it ran pell-mell up the canyon till it got here between the lodge and the river. We have some guys out there trying to catch it, but so far no luck."

"Can we watch?" Ashley asked eagerly, but her mother hushed her.

"I'm a wildlife veterinarian," Olivia said. "If there's anything I can do to help, I'd be glad to. What about darting it with a tranquilizer?"

Smiling back at her, the ranger said, "I bet you're Dr. Landon, right? I plan to come and hear you speak tomorrow."

"Right." She reached across Steven to shake the ranger's hand. "And this is my husband, Steven."

"Pleased to meet you both. Well, as far as darting her, if a tranquilizer put the mustang down, we'd have no way to drag her out. So we're trying to rope her instead. What's happening is"—he leaned his arms on the car door—"the tour-group horses that the visitors ride are corralled over there beside the lodge. This mustang seems like she wants to get near them—she keeps whinnying, and they whinny back, but every time she comes close to the corral, she gets spooked and runs away again." He looked up the road as if he were considering something, then said, "Why don't you go ahead into the parking lot, and then I'll take you to where the horse is running now. Maybe you can give us some suggestions, Dr. Landon."

"Call me Olivia. And I'd be happy to help."

The ranger pulled back the wooden barrier to let the Landons' SUV roll through. As they drove forward, Steven shook his head in pretend disapproval and said, "Did you guys see how your mother was flirting with that ranger? Shameless, isn't she?"

"Hey, it worked," Ashley answered. "He's gonna let us into the parking lot. Way to go, Mom!" Ethan just stared at his hands, but a tiny smile twitched the corners of Summer's lips. Maybe she was beginning to catch on to Steven's teasing.

They drove into a large paved area in front of a four-pillared building made of stone that matched the ginger color of the tall canyon peaks. A U.S. flag on a silvery pole hung limp in the still air. Beneath it, the vast lawn was empty of people. And there was no sign of the mustang.

"Steven, why don't you and the kids register," Olivia said, "while I try to find out what's going on with that horse."

"Wait. I want to go with you, Mom—please?" Jack pleaded.

"Me too." Ashley took Summer's hand and asked, "You want to come?"

Shyly, Summer said, "Yes." Ethan gave a terse nod.

"OK, leave the stuff in the car, and we'll all walk up," Steven said. "Just make sure you kids don't get in the way of the wranglers."

The park ranger who'd stopped them at the barrier now pointed them toward the area west of the lodge, to the other side of the road, where the Virgin River flowed, pleasant and gentle. Jack thought that the Virgin didn't look powerful enough to slice through a loaf of bread, let alone through sandstone cliffs thousands of feet high.

Several trucks with horse trailers attached were parked side by side in a half-circle on the road. As they approached, Steven peered at a man next to one of the trailers. His brow furrowed in a frown, and then he stared harder.

"Hey," he said, "I think—no, I'm sure I know that guy."

Leaving the rest of them behind, Steven ran toward a tall, grizzled man wearing a shirt with vertical stripes, jeans, and boots, and topping it all off with a huge black cowboy hat. "Len?" he called, "Len Pelton? It's you, isn't it?"

The man's mouth dropped in surprise as he shouted. "Steve? Steve-o, you young son of a gun! Well, my heck, where in thunder did you come from?"

They grabbed each other in a big bear hug with a lot of backslapping. By the time Olivia and the kids reached them, Steven was grinning so widely his eyes almost disappeared in wrinkles of glee. "This is my old group supervisor from the boys' ranch," he explained. "I started out in regular foster homes, but then the state decided it would be better for me at the ranch. At first I was scared to go, but Len—he made me feel like I belonged. I'll tell you, that was a great time for me."

"Yep, you was with me from the time you was what? Sixteen, seventeen?"

"Fifteen. And I stayed till high-school graduation," Steven answered. "So what are you doing here?"

The man raised his hat to wipe his forehead with a big handkerchief. "Workin'. Too hard, sometimes," he said, and grinned. "I'm with the Park Service now. We keep a couple of horses here in Zion for search-and-rescue operations and for jobs like this one. What happened today was—a couple of lady ranchers adopted a wild mustang from the Bureau of Land Management. They was drivin' through the park this mornin' and stopped at the visitor center for a hour or so, when the pin on their trailer door worked loose, and the horse busted out."

Again the brim of the hat got tilted back; this time Len scratched the top of his balding head.

"The mustang was adopted, you said?" Steven asked, encouraging Len to go on with the story.

"Yep, you know how the BLM adopts out wild mustangs every now and then. This one's a young mare, and she's been leadin' us a merry dance. I'm wore out from chasin' her. Ain't as young as I once was." Len laughed and patted his round belly; it bulged over the big silver buckle on his belt. Then he said, "Hey, Steve-o, wanna try her?"

"Try what?"

"Catchin' the mustang. For old times' sake. When I had you at the boys' ranch, you was the best wrangler I ever seen in all my years there. I told you you ought to go on the rodeo circuit, but you got interested in those dang cameras instead. So now, here's your chance to show if you still got the stuff in you to catch a horse."

"Steven, I really don't think you should—" Olivia began.

"And who's this pretty little lady?" Len interrupted, his voice booming.

"This is my wife, Olivia. And these are my kids." Steven's outflung arm included Summer and Ethan, who hung back. But for once, Ethan looked interested.

"Hey, go for it, Dad!" Jack yelled. "I want to see you ride."

"You can take this here gelding, Steve," Len told him, pointing to a tall horse tied up to a roadside sign-post. "He's saddled and ready to go. Here's a couple of ropes. The wild mare's down there beside the river somewheres—you'll see the other two riders workin' her. We're tryin' to get her before she heads back up to the lodge again."

"You mean you want Steven to ride down there on all those rocks and try to rope a wild horse?" Olivia asked, her voice rising.

"We gotta get her out of here," Len replied. "If we can't rope her, we might have to shoot her."

Ashley gasped, and Jack felt his stomach squeeze tight. "Why can't you just leave her here in the park to run wild?" he asked.

"She's an exotic. Look," Len said, "there's no time now to explain park policy. We gotta get that mustang while there's still daylight. These here canyon walls are so tall that once the sun gets behind 'em, it'll be too dark to chase down a horse, even if it's only five in the afternoon. What do you say, Steve-o? Wanna do 'er?"

"I'm ready and willin'." All of a sudden Steven didn't sound like the father Jack knew; he was talking more like Len. Like a ranch hand. Before Jack knew it, Steven had swung himself up on the back of the tall brown-and-white horse. "What's his name?" he asked, leaning forward in the saddle to stroke the horse's neck.

"Glory Hallelujah. My grandkid named him. But we call him Hal."

Nudging Hal with his knee, Steven moved the horse to the shoulder of the paved road, where he paused, looking for an easy descent down the slope to the river. Chunks of rock of all different shapes, from breadbox-size to Volkswagen-size, littered the slope and the bed of the Virgin River. Jack and Ashley, excited, crowded the edge of the road to watch their father. Summer and Ethan watched, too, while Olivia stood beside them, nervously chewing her thumbnail. "I'm scared. It's been years since he did anything like this," she murmured.

Jack watched intently as his father rode upriver to where two other men on horseback were talking to one another. At the back of his mind hung a question he wanted to ask his mother when all this was over. Len had said the runaway wild mare was an exotic. Jack pretty much knew what that meant. If a species invaded an environment where it didn't belong, it was called an exotic species. Like the wild boars at Hawaii Volcanoes National Park. The boars weren't native to the Hawaiian Islands; they were brought there by the first Polynesian settlers. When they ran wild, they dug up palm tree roots and destroyed the trees. In Florida, people brought iguanas as pets from Mexico and sometimes turned them loose; a few of them escaped into Everglades National Park, where they multiplied. Wild boars and iguanas sounded like exotic species, but a horse? A plain old horse?

Steven reached the other men and spoke to them. Jack couldn't hear what they said, but he saw them gesturing to a rocky rise above them. There she stood, the mustang mare, a gray color so pale it was almost white, making her look silver in the sunlight. Her sides were heaving from exertion, or maybe from fear.

"She has a name," Len told them. "She's called Mariah."

"'They call the wind Mariah,'" Ashley murmured. "She looks like the wind."

"She looks like a ghost," Summer said, low enough that Jack wasn't sure he'd heard her. The horse did look ghostly, pale against the red rock, her black mane falling over her forehead. She whinnied as though calling her herd for help, but she was all alone.

Then Jack's eyes jerked back to his father, because Steven had ridden forward, a coiled rope in one hand, the other hand guiding the horse named Hal. They picked their way carefully past the rocks, sometimes splashing through the shallow Virgin River. Just as slowly, the other two men moved away from Steven, one stopping in front of Mariah, the second riding farther upriver. Mariah stood still on her rock outcropping, snorting, wide-eyed, her ears laid back, moving her head from side to side to watch all three riders.

"Be careful, Steven," Olivia said, barely breathing the words.

Suddenly Steven sent his horse into a gallop, climbing the steep incline toward Mariah. She looked for a path to escape, but the other two riders were heading toward her from other directions. The rope in Steven's hand took shape as if by magic, spinning in a perfect circle. Whinnying and turning, Mariah reared up just as Steven tossed the loop of his rope over her head. When she jerked her neck back violently, the taut rope nearly pulled Steven off his own horse. Both Hal and the silvery mustang danced backward and then forward on the slope as small rocks, loosened by their hooves, rolled down toward the river.

"No!" Olivia cried as Steven's horse began to slip on the loose rocks, its hooves thrashing wildly. Steven fought hard to keep both his balance and his control of Hal, at the same time wrapping the taut rope around Hal's saddle horn.

"Steady, boy, hold 'em steady," Len yelled. But Hal slipped even more dangerously on the sharp incline.

"He's falling!" Ashley screamed. "If the horse lands on Daddy, he'll—"

Jack clapped his hand over his sister's mouth to shut her up. It was scary enough without Ashley screaming. Across the river, Hal's rear legs buckled beneath him as he flung his head in panic. Steven struggled mightily while both horses pulled in opposite directions.

The other riders tried to find a way to reach him through the rough terrain, but Steven didn't need any help. He managed to quiet Hal, get him upright on all fours, and hang onto Mariah at the same time, leading both horses to the safer flat land along the riverbanks.

"What a rider!" Len yelled. "Good as he ever was! That boy always did have a natural-born talent for handlin' horses. If he ever gets tired of that photography business and wants a real job—"

Jack kept cheering, "Way to go, Dad!" while Steven rode across the shallow Virgin River, leading a balky Mariah by the rope around her neck. Steven must have felt pretty good about what he'd done, too, because halfway across, he let out a loud, "Yee haw!"

Laughing, feeling so proud of his father he could burst, Jack turned toward Ethan and Summer. They were standing with their heads close together, whispering. Neither of them looked one bit relieved or happy that Steven was safe. Instead, Summer looked…worried!

CHAPTER FOUR

Jack thought his mother was going to run up to his father and hug him or something because he'd been in so much danger. If Hal had fallen on him, Steven could have been crushed.

Instead, Olivia moved straight for Mariah, slowly, carefully approaching the frightened horse. Mariah reared back, choking for air as the rope tightened around her neck. "It's OK, it's OK," Olivia kept saying in a soft, soothing voice while Len, working swiftly, managed to get a halter on the mustang. Cautiously, Olivia raised her hand to stroke Mariah's silvery neck, and then gently rubbed the spot just above the horse's jaw. "Good horse, good horse," she kept murmuring.

Len said to the kids, "Looks like your mom's got a way with horses, too, just like your dad does."

"She's a wildlife veterinarian," Jack told him.

"Well, my heck!" Len exclaimed. "I shoulda figured

that one out by myself. She's Dr. Olivia Landon, right? She's gonna speak at the seminar tomorrow about how we handle animals in the park. Hey, Art," he yelled to one of the two riders crossing the river toward them, "that pretty lady is—guess who? Dr. Landon!"

Jack couldn't help himself—he had to turn around and toss a cocky grin at Ethan. Jack's dad had just proved he could handle a horse like a champion; his mother was being treated like a celebrity. Since Jack had exceptionally cool parents, that trickled down to make *him* special, too. Ethan just stood, his face as stony as usual, his legs planted into the ground like two trees.

Steven and the other two men had dismounted and were holding their horses by the reins. "I'm Art Meacham," one of the men said, introducing himself to Olivia, "from the Bureau of Land Management, and this is Gus Todd, also from BLM." After the introductions, Art mentioned, "Soon as we get these horses back into the trailers, I'd sure like it if we'd all go into the lodge for a soda. I'll buy, Steven, since we owe you big time for ropin' Mariah here."

"Will she be all right?" Olivia asked, concerned about the frosty, almost white mustang that snorted and pawed at the ground. Mariah's dark eyes were opened wide enough to show the whites all around.

"She's just scared, but she'll quiet down," Art answered. "We've had her in a corral at the BLM holding facilities for the past couple of months, so she's lost a lot of her wildness. She still put on quite a show for us, though." He paused, then said, "Hey, I guess I better radio headquarters so they can tell those ladies we got their horse. After we grab our drink, I'll haul Mariah back down to the visitor center."

In the lodge coffee shop, they settled into chairs— the five grown-ups around one table, the four kids at another table right next to them. Both Art and Gus were dressed pretty much the same as Len, in typical Western clothes: plaid shirts, thick leather belts with big silver-and-turquoise buckles, Levis, and boots. At the table, out of politeness to the lady—Olivia—they'd taken off their wide-brimmed cowboy hats. All three of them wore their hair cut short; their necks looked tanned and leathery, like old boots.

"Man, did you see my dad?" Jack enthused as he slid into his seat. "I couldn't believe he did that! I never knew he could ride—not like that, anyhow."

"Well, I hope he never does it again," Ashley snapped.

"Why?"

"Duh! Because that big horse nearly fell on him."

"You worry too much," Jack answered with a grin. "Dad's tough. What did you think, Ethan? I mean, about my dad riding all that muscle and energy—it's got to be awesome to rope that kind of power and bring it under control. You know, I bet he could break Mariah a lot faster than the new owners will. Maybe he can tell them how it's done."

Ethan picked a paper-covered straw out of a metal container and began to peel the tissue away, dropping bits of it onto the table like flakes of snow. Without looking up, he said, "The Shoshone respect horses."

"Yeah," Jack nodded, "I like them, too."

"Not the same way. We don't break their spirits."

"What do you mean? If you want to ride a horse, you've got to break it first. Show it who's boss. That doesn't mean hurting their spirits or anything. Don't your people ride horses?"

"Shoshone are the best riders anywhere. But we're partners with the horse. We don't need to be master."

The excitement of the roundup was starting to seep out of Jack. Leaning back in his chair, he eyed Ethan. "So, now you're saying white folks hurt wild horses?"

Ethan pressed his fists against the table. "Grand-mother told us white people try to conquer anything that gets in their way. Listen to what you said—you want to 'break' Mariah. 'Control' her. That's not what we do. Shoshone people honor their horses."

"So you think my dad should have left Mariah alone?" Jack asked, his voice rising. "That way, she might have been shot dead instead. Would that have honored her?"

"Mr. Landon is a cowboy. They're all cowboys." With a toss of his head, he indicated the men sitting at the next table. "It's Cowboys against Indians."

Summer quickly scooted her chair closer to her brother. "Ethan, do you want a root beer?" she asked at the same time Jack felt a tug on his T-shirt sleeve. Ashley was trying to get his attention in the same way Summer was trying to get Ethan's, but Jack refused to look at his sister until she put her face right in front of his. "Will you guys stop?" she hissed. "I'm trying to listen to Mom and Dad. They've been talking about Mariah, and I want to hear."

"Sure," Jack agreed. "I don't have anything more to say."

Ethan and Jack stared at each another, eyes locked, as the conversation from the next table filtered over to theirs.

"…here for your meeting tomorrow," Art was saying to Olivia, "which is why I was lucky enough to be on the scene for the roundup. The park wants to keep everything natural, with no interference from humans. But we folks at the BLM have to manage rangeland so the ranchers can graze their cattle there, and at the same time preserve and protect wild mustangs like Mariah. Sometimes those two goals clash."

"You mean crash together like a train wreck," Gus added. "You know, Dr. Landon—"

"Remember, call me Olivia."

"Right. Anyway, Olivia, there's an interesting story about that horse Mariah that you took such a likin' to just now. She belongs to the Chloride herd that runs on the range about 30 miles from our headquarters. We had to thin out that herd because the ranchers complained the wild mustangs eat too much grass."

Len Pelton broke in, "Two and a half million cattle graze on BLM land in the West, and only 46,000 mustangs, but the mustangs supposedly eat too much. Go figure."

"Well, like I said," Gus went on, "when we captured Mariah, there was another white horse with her, a mare. Looked just like Mariah, only several years older; I'm judging that Mariah's about three now. Maybe the older one was Mariah's mother, 'cause the two of them seemed real close, touching and whinnying when we penned them together in the corral. But the next morning, the older horse turned up dead. Her neck was broke."

Beside Jack, Summer gave a quick little gasp.

"Why? What happened?" Olivia asked.

"Looked like she ran full-tilt into the panels of the corral. Horses' necks are fragile; it happens sometimes. But she must have hit that panel at top speed, like—a suicide. It's a mystery why she done that. And then— it happened again."

"The same thing? Again? Tell me," Olivia demanded.

Gus scraped back his chair and leaned forward. "See, the horses of the Chloride herd do behave kind of peculiar. No one knows why they act so strange. They whinny a lot more than most mustangs, and they do a lot of stuff I've never seen horses do before. Some of the local folks are even afraid of 'em, tellin' scary stories about that herd."

"Like that newspaper fellow," Art said, rubbing the faint stubble on his chin.

"That man had no more sense than a rock," Len added with a shake of his head.

Gus nodded slowly. "What turns my crank is that I told that reporter fellow what happened to Mariah's mom. Told him not to try to trap a white horse since we lost one that way. Didn't make a whit of difference. Mr. Reporter wanted a story, so he did what he did."

With intense interest, Olivia looked from one weathered face to another.

"See, Olivia," Art broke in, "a couple of months ago this newspaper guy hears about our ghost horses and decides to see for himself. He hides in the bush, waiting until one goes inside a trap. Luckily, it was just one—all by itself. Well, as soon as he slams the gate shut, the ghost horse starts acting crazy, banging against the panels just like Mariah's mom did."

"And then the dang fool runs off and leaves it!" Gus finished. "By the time we found out about it, it was too late. Another dead mustang, all because some reporter wouldn't listen."

"So what do you make of all of these stories about the ghost horses?" Olivia pressed.

Art studied his fingernails. "I don't pay them no

mind," he said finally, "but still, there's something spooky about those white horses—"

At that, Summer clutched her brother's arm, but Ethan just shook his head to signal her to remain silent.

Art broke in suddenly, "Why don't you come on out and see those mustangs, Olivia? You're the expert. How about it?"

"Hmmm, spooky white horses that whinny and touch each other a lot and kill themselves by running into wall panels. Sounds like mysterious behavior. You say the herd's called the Chloride?"

"Yes ma'am. Named after the canyon where they run, past Cedar City."

Nodding, Olivia said, "OK, you're on. I think I'd like to get a look at these unusual mustangs."

Ashley couldn't contain herself any longer. Jumping up, she begged, "Can we go too? Jack and Ethan and Summer and me?"

Jack held his breath, hoping his mother would say yes. Even though he sent her an appealing look, Olivia still shook her head no, telling them that it was too big an imposition for Gus, since there were too many of them, and it was far out in the wild country—

Gus interrupted with, "Hey, I'd be happy to take the whole kit and caboodle of you folks. The real question's how patient the kids are. We're gonna try to trap a few more of the Chloride mustangs tomorrow night, but it means waiting by the water hole, sometimes for hours and hours. And you can't talk or move when the horses get close, 'cause it'll spook them."

"We're patient," Jack said eagerly, "and Summer and Ethan hardly talk at all. The only yacky one is my sister—"

"*Jack!*" Ashley protested.

"You want to come, don't you, Summer? Wouldn't you like to see the ghost horses?" Steven asked.

"Say yes!" Ashley told Summer, grabbing her hand.

"Yes." But the word sounded soft and uncertain.

Neither Jack nor Ashley asked Ethan whether he wanted to watch: In the excitement, none of the adults seemed to notice him.

"Well, sounds like we got a plan," Art and Gus agreed. "We better get Mariah back to those two ranch ladies now, since they're probably wantin' to get on their way home."

After the good-byes were said, the Landons began to unpack their luggage from the SUV. "That was an exciting start to our trip, catching the mustang and meeting those guys," Steven commented. "Now we'd better lug this stuff up to our rooms and then get some dinner. Look how dark it is already in this canyon. Len was right. Once the sun gets behind these canyon walls, everything's in shadow."

Ethan objected strongly when he was told he had to share a room with Jack. "Why can't I stay in the same room with my sister?" he asked.

"We think it's better for the boys to be in one room and the girls in another," Steven explained.

Hey, it's not like I want to be in a room with *you,* either, Jack thought. While they unpacked, both boys stayed silent, avoiding eye contact, and kept as far apart from each other as the small room would allow. It was going to be a long couple of days.

Dinner at the lodge restaurant was a quiet affair, with each of them lost in thought. As they finished their desserts, Ashley asked, "Can we dance the Ghost Dance again tonight?"

"No," Summer answered, but Ethan said more loudly, "Yes. We need to find another cedar tree, and we need to wear blankets. It's part of the magic."

"I'm not dancing this time," Jack announced.

"You said you would!" Ashley protested. "Yesterday, at the cemetery, you said—"

"I changed my mind."

Carefully folding his napkin, Steven began, "Um— I don't think the lodge would appreciate it if you kids took the blankets off the beds and carried them outside. How about towels? Would that work?" When Ethan reluctantly agreed, Steven continued, "So why don't you three go and get the things you need for the dance. I want to talk to Jack for a minute, and then we'll join you."

CHAPTER FIVE

Glancing at his father, Jack waited. Steven looked tired. The skin under his eyes was shadowed, and his shoulders seemed to slump. Straightening himself, he said, "Son, I know you don't want to do this dance tonight, but I'd like you to make things as easy for Ethan as you can. If he wants to share some of his Shoshone background with you, then you ought to be happy about it. Culture exchange can be a rewarding, two-way street."

"Culture exchange?" Jack exploded. "That's a joke. You don't know what it's like being stuck with him— he's always grumbling about something, saying white people are bad and all kinds of stuff. Why am I the one who has to go along? Why don't you make Ethan do what *I* want?"

"Jack, I want you to step back from the situation and realize something. You have been given everything.

You've got parents who love you, a comfortable home—Ethan's needs are far greater than yours are right now. You may not know what it feels like to have everything taken from you, but I do. So I'm asking you…." He sighed, then continued, "Would you please try?"

"We've all got to give a little here," his mother added, placing her spoon and knife in perfect alignment with her plate on the tablecloth. "The truth is, your father and I would rather call it a night right now—we're both tired, and I have a big day ahead of me tomorrow. But the dance seems to be important to Ethan; therefore, by extension, it's important to all of us. Can you be a good sport and go along with it once more?"

Jack looked at the wooden walls, which had been coated in a thick varnish that cast a golden glow throughout the restaurant. He knew his parents were right, even though he didn't want to admit it. He needed to remember how it would feel to be Ethan, to walk around in his world, or as the saying that he'd heard so many times went, to walk a mile in his moccasins. Maybe Jack would have turned out the exact same way if he'd been raised the way Ethan had. Still, doing the right thing was hard.

Yet there was something more—something that tugged at his mind, something that whispered that maybe he ought to give in and dance once again with Summer and Ethan. Yesterday, at the top of the Shoshone cemetery where a stark gray monument honored Sacagawea, Jack had danced the Ghost Dance. And while he danced, he'd smelled smoke from burning trees. Only there weren't any trees burning, not on the entire Wind River Reservation. He remembered how weird it was. If he danced tonight, would he smell smoke again?

He frowned, which made his parents look at him questioningly. No, it must have been his imagination yesterday, triggered by Summer's grandmother's grandmother's story. Forget it. Jack faced his parents and said, "All right."

"Thanks, son," his dad told him. "Here come the other kids now."

Ashley thrust a towel at Jack and said, "I brought you one anyway. I figured maybe you'd change your mind again."

"I guess. Thanks," he said, folding it over his arm. The towels provided by the lodge weren't very large— Zion Lodge was nice, but not the kind of luxury hotel where the bath towels were as big as beach towels. Jack didn't know why they had to wear them anyway. Pretending the towels were Indian blankets seemed pretty stupid to him, but he'd told his parents he'd cooperate, so the best thing he could do would be to go along and get it over with. It just gave Ethan another chance to show off, with his hey-ya ya-ha stuff that he probably made up as he went along.

When they got outside, Jack caught his breath. A

huge full moon rose over the red cliffs, casting moon shadows on the front lawn of Zion Lodge. He wished he could take a picture of the scene, but without a wide-angle lens, his camera couldn't begin to capture that canopy of nighttime splendor.

"There's a cedar tree," Ethan said, gesturing toward the center of the lawn.

"You know, they're not really cedars," Jack said, "even though people around here call them that. They're actually junipers."

"Whatever," Ethan muttered, tossing his head. His hair swung thick and black and long in the moonlight.

While Olivia and Steven sat nearby on the grass, the four kids wrapped their towels across their shoulders like blankets.

"I don't think these will stay on when we dance," Ashley worried.

"They'll stay," Ethan told her.

They took one another's hands just as they had the day before, but for some reason the Ghost Dance felt different at night. Ethan chanted the same song—at least Jack guessed it was the same, but since he couldn't understand the words, he couldn't be sure. The dance seemed to go on and on until Jack started getting tired of shuffling his feet and circling the cedar tree, which loomed dark in the night shadows. Every few minutes he sniffed the slight breeze that cooled their faces, but he couldn't smell even a whiff of smoke. So, yesterday had been nothing but his imagination.

They'd had a long day today, first flying from Jackson Hole, Wyoming, to the St. George, Utah, airport, then driving the distance to the park, and then all those other things that had happened. Ethan and Summer should have been tired, too, but they just kept dancing, and so did Ashley. Jack wasn't going to be the first one to admit he wanted to quit.

Finally it was Olivia who called a halt. "We need to get to bed—or anyway I do," she said. "Tomorrow will start early for me."

"One more thing before we stop dancing," Ethan instructed them. "We're supposed to take off the blankets and shake them like this. It's part of the magic."

"They're not blankets, they're just towels," Jack mumbled, but he shook his anyway, trying to copy Ethan.

"Can't we stay up a little longer?" Ashley pleaded. "We always tell stories around the campfire when we're in a park—"

Steven said wryly, "I don't think the lodge owners would appreciate it if we built a fire on their lawn."

That wasn't enough to deflect Ashley, who could always burrow her way around an obstacle. "We'll just use the cedar tree and pretend it's a fire," she suggested. But Steven and Olivia were already standing up, preparing to herd the kids inside.

Shyly, Summer said, "I know a story."

It was so unexpected that everyone paused, silent for a moment. Jack felt sure that his mother wouldn't make them leave now, not since Summer had actually volunteered to take part in this perfect September evening under a star-filled sky—or as much of the sky as showed between the narrow canyon walls. He was right: Olivia hesitated, then smiled at Summer and said, "That would be lovely."

"Maybe it's not a story," Summer said. "Maybe it's a poem."

"Even better," Olivia told her. They arranged their towels on the grass and sat in a little half circle, Ethan far enough away from the Landons to show he didn't want to be part of the family.

Standing in front of them all, slowly moving from one foot to the other as she spoke, Summer began her tale in a voice so singsong it might actually have been a song:

Long ago, our legends told
Of a horse no one could tame,
Her sire, they say, was the devil himself,
Wild Spirit was her name.

Wild Spirit danced upon the wind,
Luring many with her magic,
But those who tried to ride her
faced a death both cruel and tragic.

Though men would dream of snaring her,
Wild Spirit galloped free,
Her mane flowed loose, her hoofbeats roared
Across untamed prairie.

'Til a Shoshone woman with sun-baked hands
Heard the legend, and the story
Of the renegade horse, of the path she ran,
Of Wild Spirit's savage glory.

To the high mountain the woman climbed,
And when she heard loud thunder
Cracking through a clear blue sky,
She felt both fear and wonder.

Out of the mist the horse appeared,
Its eyes were wild as lightning,
Never before had the woman seen
A savage beast so frightening.

The woman stood like a cedar tree
Against those eyes of fire,
Softly she questioned the specter's rage
As the smoky mane whirled higher.

"My realm is gone!" the fierce horse roared,
"White men have bled my earth,"
"I too have lost," the woman wept,
"Cut from my land of birth."

They looked into each other's eyes
And saw a mirror there,
The grief of losing both their worlds
Had laid their two souls bare.

Now legend tells of a ghostly horse,
Stars paint Wild Spirit's track,
They light a path though the velvet sky,
And a woman rides her back.

Jack didn't know whether he should applaud, and it seemed no one else knew, either. It would be like applauding a hymn in church. Then, softly, Olivia said, "That was beautiful, Summer. Where did you learn that poem?"

"From Grandmother."

"Did your grandmother make up the poem?" Ashley asked.

"I don't know—she just used to say it." Summer's eyes brimmed with tears. Hunching her shoulders, she crossed her arms across her chest as if to hug herself, then retreated again into silence.

It was then that Jack heard it, the whinnying of a horse in the distance. A ghost horse! The hair stood up on his arms.

Wait a minute, he told himself. Earlier that afternoon, the ranger had mentioned that horses were stabled next to the lodge, to take tourists on guided rides through the park. That must be what he heard.

But the whinnying didn't come from behind him, where the lodge was. He heard it across the river, high in the sandstone cliffs. Rubbing his arms, he tried to reason it out. Probably the whinnying started in the stables next to the lodge, but the sound flew across the canyon to bounce off the rock walls and echo back at him. That was it—an echo. Sure. Perfectly logical. Nothing but an echo. But didn't anyone else hear it?

Ethan stood up and said, "Summer gave us a gift of the poem. Now we're supposed to give her something."

"What?" Jack asked, stuffing his hands into the pockets of his jeans to see if he had anything there. All he found was a little bag of peanuts from the airplane ride that morning. Solemnly, he handed it to Summer. Olivia located a pack of gum in her sweatshirt pocket. Steven held out a wrapped peppermint he'd picked up on his way out of the restaurant. Ashley offered a flower—a delicate purple aster. Maybe the lodge owner wouldn't like it that Ashley picked the flower from a border that had been planted along the front steps, but hey, Jack was too puzzled about the echo to worry about it, and his parents didn't say anything to Ashley.

Summer seemed pleased with their small gifts. She slipped them into the pocket of her sundress, except for the flower. That she wound into one of her long black braids.

CHAPTER SIX

Your mom left a long time ago," Steven told his son.

Barefoot, tousle-haired, still in his sleep shirt, Jack had wandered through the connecting door to his parents' room in the lodge. His dad, fully dressed, said, "She had to get to the seminar, but she didn't want me to wake you boys since you were up so late last night."

"Ethan's already awake," Jack told him. "He was looking out the window, and when I asked him if he liked Zion National Park, you know what he said, Dad?"

"What?"

"He said all of Yellowstone National Park used to be Shoshone land, but the government robbed it from them and paid the Shoshone, like, two cents an acre or something like that. Do you think that could be true?"

Steven took a deep breath and let it out slowly. "Sad to say—yes, I think it could be true. Lots of, uh, less than honorable dealings have happened in our government's history with the Native Americans."

Wow, Jack thought, no wonder Ethan doesn't like Anglos very much. But still, that was then and this was now. None of the Landons had taken Yellowstone away from Ethan and his tribe. Besides, what could anyone do about it now? Aloud, he said, "I'm hungry. Where are we going to eat?"

"Downstairs in the restaurant. Get dressed and bring Ethan with you. The girls are already down there."

Smells of bacon and the faint scent of vanilla met Jack as he made his way up the long staircase from the lobby and into the dining area. Dishes clattered and servers rushed by, intent on carrying food to their customers. It took only a few minutes for Jack to spy Ashley, who was having an intense conversation with Summer. That is, Ashley was intense—Summer just watched and nodded, emotionless. Yet her lack of expression could be deceiving, since she always seemed to absorb everything Ashley said.

"Where's my sister?" Ethan asked brusquely.

"Over there," Steven answered, pointing. "Looks like they already ordered hot chocolate, complete with whipped cream. You can order some too, if you like."

After they'd settled into the wooden chairs, Steven asked for coffee and then turned to the four of them. His long arms rested on the polished tabletop like two bent tree limbs, while his fingers knit together. "Well, now, what would you kids like to do today?"

"Anything," Ashley answered.

"Your mom's going to be busy with the seminar until late afternoon, which leaves us plenty of time to see the park. I thought maybe while we're waiting for her, we could all go on a hike. There's lots of trails that start out here at the lodge."

Jack and Ashley agreed enthusiastically. Ethan and Summer exchanged glances.

"I don't want to go. Neither does Summer," Ethan said stiffly. Summer dropped her lids as her brother went on, "Ever since you picked us up, you've told us what we are going to do. Me and Summer don't want to hike."

"I can understand that, Ethan. Do you mind telling me why?" Steven glanced at their feet, then asked, "Is it because you two are in tennis shoes? That doesn't have to be a problem—we can stay on the paved trails."

Ashley frowned down at her own hiking boots. Jack knew what his sister was thinking—why should Jack and Ashley have sturdy mountain boots when the two foster kids wore scuffed, frayed sneakers? Fortunately Ashley's feet were bigger than Summer's and smaller than Ethan's; otherwise, Jack knew, she'd rip off her boots and give them to the Ingawanup kids. Ashley was like that.

"What would you like to do, Ethan?" Steven wanted to know.

"I don't know. Stay in our room, I guess."

"You've got to be kidding," Jack sputtered. "We're

in *Zion!* Look out the window—do you want to miss all this? Come *on!*"

"Go without us. We'll stay here."

Steven gave Jack a look, and then answered, "Ethan, we can't leave you. We've all got to stick together. Summer, what would you like to do?"

"She wants to stay here with me," Ethan said through tight lips. But Summer shook her head, her chin thrust out in a way that for once appeared stubborn. "No, Ethan. I spent my whole life on Wind River Reservation, and now I have a chance to see this park. I want to go."

"Summer, you know what Grandmother always said," Ethan began hotly.

"Grandmother would want us to see what the Great Spirit has made," Summer countered.

"But—"

"Ethan, I did the Ghost Dance, even when I thought it was bad. You know I always do what you say. Now I'm asking you to come with me." A beat later, she added, "Please."

Even though Ethan didn't answer Summer, Jack could tell when he agreed to go. It was almost as if the Ingawanup brother and sister could speak to each other with only a flick of their eyes, a nod, that wasn't really a nod and a glance that was no more than smoke. They would go. Relieved, Jack looked out across the lawn and into the rose-tipped peaks, vowing to himself that he wouldn't let Ethan get the better of him on this hike. No matter how tired or thirsty he became, Jack decided he was going to stay at least one pace ahead of Ethan.

"OK. I'm going." Ethan stared at Jack while he said that through clenched jaws. For some unknown reason, he chose that moment to pull his long black hair into a ponytail, securing it with a rubber band. Was that supposed to mean something, like he was preparing for combat?

They started out with granola bars and bottled water divided between Jack's and Ashley's backpacks. Jack kept his camera in a special flap in his pack; if the chocolate coating on the granola bars melted, he didn't want it to smear his lens. His dad carried a much bigger pack filled with much better and considerably more expensive camera equipment. As a professional photographer, Steven was always eager to capture any outstanding shots he might come across.

"Where are we going, Dad?" Ashley asked when they were ready to leave.

Steven unfolded a map and lowered it so all the kids could follow his finger as he traced a trail. "We'll head up toward The Narrows. When we get here,"—he pointed to a spot called the Grotto—"we'll cross a footbridge and get onto this West Rim trail. After that we'll just hike as long as we want to, or until somebody gets too tired."

As they hiked along the trail paralleling the Virgin River, Ethan and Summer hung back behind the other three. Often, Steven turned and paused, waiting for the Ingawanup kids to catch up. After a mile they crossed a footbridge to the west side of the river. On that side, as on the east side, the Virgin's placid flow had allowed cottonwoods and box elder trees to flourish, a startling green against the red rock. From the trail, they had a magnificent view of the Great White Throne, a megalith of Navajo sandstone that was white on the top half and red at the base. It towered above the peaks around it.

"That's one of the best-known mountains in the United States," Steven told them. "Its picture was on a postage stamp once. So now I'm going to take a picture of it, too."

While Steven set up his tripod, Jack pulled out his own camera. It would be hard to take a bad picture of the Great White Throne, but he decided to wait until they were on their way back from wherever they were hiking. By then, the sun would be above the peak, not behind it and making a silhouette, the way it was now.

"Want to see?" he asked Summer, offering her his camera. "Put your eye here, and you can tell what your picture will look like."

Summer held the camera, peering into the small square viewfinder until Ethan grabbed it from her to hand it back to Jack. Summer didn't protest, but fell into step behind her brother.

By the time they'd gone one mile past the footbridge, they'd climbed a thousand feet higher in elevation. Steven and the Landon kids were not even panting, although Jack's throat felt as dry as dust. He kept glancing at Ethan, checking for a sign of weakness, but Ethan moved as effortlessly along the trail as if he were on a carpeted floor. Ahead of them loomed another monolith called Angels Landing.

"Anyone want to quit?" Steven asked. "The trail guide says it gets a lot steeper from here on. Ethan, Summer—you guys OK?"

Summer and Ethan eyed Ashley and Jack—maybe the Ingawanup kids were doing some checking of their own. Three of them answered all at once, "Let's go." "Don't want to quit." "No problem." Ethan just stood still, his head craned back, watching a small bird swoop through the sky like a silvery arrow searching for its mark.

The trail guidebook was right—the climb got a *whole* lot steeper. At this elevation, autumn came a little earlier; it had tinted the leaves of the big-toothed maples, turning them close to the color of the red sandstone walls. As they got near the head of the canyon, Jack burst out, "What the heck is that up ahead?"

Twenty-one separate switchbacks zigzagged up the face of the canyon, like a bolt of lightning carved into rock. Stone walls, the same color as the red sandstone, held the switchbacks in place to keep them from sliding down the sheer slope. Even the concrete that paved the trails had been dyed a ruddy color to blend with the canyon walls.

Steven leafed through his guidebook and said, "They're called Walters Wiggles."

"Walter's what?" Ashley asked, giggling and swiveling her skinny hips from side to side. "Like this?"

"Yeah, Wiggles. It says they were carved out of the rock in 1926 by Park Service crews, then the trail was improved in the 1930s by young kids not much older than you guys, who belonged to the CCC—the Civilian Conservation Corps. That was during the Depression. The CCC gave paying jobs to kids who otherwise would have been broke, hungry, and homeless."

"Whew! Hauling out rocks on that steep trail? I think I'd rather starve," Jack said.

"No you wouldn't." Ethan's words had a hard edge. "You don't know nothin' about starving."

"I bet you don't either," Jack shot back.

"But my grandmother did. She knew about starving. She taught us to be tough. She taught us to be brave." Ethan grabbed Summer's hand and hurried ahead of the Landons, moving fast up the switchback trail.

"Hey, you two, slow down," Steven yelled. "It's a big climb."

"Let them go," Jack said, rubbing his calf to work out a cramp in his muscle, as he decided for the second time in two days that competing with Ethan in hill climbing just wasn't worth the effort. "I'm getting kind of sick of him, anyway. Besides, we'll catch up."

Summer and Ethan stood waiting for the Landons at the top of Walters Wiggles. Summer looked tired. Ethan was wearing his usual stony expression, yet in his eyes Jack detected a look of triumph. Jack wanted to gulp for air—it had been a hard climb for sure, and he was sweating—but he slowed his breathing to as close to normal as he could manage.

"Maybe we'd better turn back here," Steven told everyone. "After this it gets *really* tough."

"No. I want to keep going," Ethan said.

"I thought you didn't want to hike at all," Jack shot back.

"I didn't. But as long as I'm here, I'll master this mountain. Unless *you're* too tired to keep going." Ethan's lip curled in the suggestion of a smirk.

"No way," Jack declared, running his fingers through sweat-dampened hair.

"Well, *I* want to stop here and take a couple of pictures," Steven announced. He didn't seem to mind that Ethan could see him panting. Pulling a white handkerchief from his pocket, Steven rubbed the back of his neck and turned toward the valley. The view, from that high elevation all the way down to the canyon floor, was incredible. Far beneath them, the Virgin River wound through the rocks and trees like a silvery snake in a narrow piece of green carpet.

"We'll meet you up above," Ethan declared. "Come on, Summer."

"*Stupid,*" Jack said under his breath, while Steven muttered, "OK, I guess I'll take this scene on the way down. I don't want those two mountain goats to get too far ahead." By the time Steven had jammed his camera back into his pack, Summer and Ethan looked doll-size in the distance. "Ethan, Summer—wait up!" Steven yelled. His voice echoed lightly off the rock face as he shouted again, "Wait up!" Jack listened for any reply, but there was none. One more time, Steven cupped his hands around his mouth to yell, but when his words died, there was nothing but silence.

Annoyed, Steven pressed his lips together, then said, "Come on, kids, it looks like Ethan's turned this into some kind of race. Let's go."

The trail angled southeast, following a ridge toward Angels Landing. Heavy chains had been attached to the rock to serve as handrails alongside the deadly drop-offs. "You guys hang onto these chains," Steven instructed. "Summer! Ethan! Quit hiking. Hold on to the chains and wait for us!" But the Ingawanup kids were still nowhere to be seen. They seemed to have vanished into the thin mountain air.

Suddenly Jack heard a loud crack and a rumble. It couldn't be thunder, because the sky was clear blue. The rumble became a crashing, and—

"Get back!" Steven yelled, pushing Jack and Ashley

hard against the sheer wall. A fist-size rock bounced down from overhead. *"Stay* back!" Steven yelled even louder. "More's coming!"

As the three of them flattened themselves against the canyon wall, pebbles rolled down, too small to do harm but stinging just the same. The pebbles bounced on their shoulders as tiny bits of grit peppered their hair. The rumbling grew louder, like a crack of thunder. A boulder the size of a basketball caromed off a small outcropping only a yard above Steven's head. It arced out to land on the path below, where it rolled until it stopped against a mound of sand and small rocks. "Don't move till we're sure there's no more," Steven shouted, flinging out his arm to hold Ashley immobile.

For what seemed like ages they stayed there, pressed against the sheer slickrock. Then they heard the sound of more pounding, only this time it was the pounding of feet as Ethan and Summer ran down the trail toward them. "Are you all right?" Summer cried. Ethan's eyes looked as hard as the rocks that had almost killed them.

He did this, Jack thought suddenly. The thought scoured into him, making his insides raw with fury. It was obvious—Ethan had run ahead, and then there was an avalanche that could have killed them all, and he didn't even care enough to look concerned. *He* rolled those rocks down on us. The spit dried in Jack's mouth as he stared Ethan down.

"Some kids—" Summer panted. "I saw them. Teenagers. They left the trail and tried to climb up the slope. They kicked the rocks loose—I don't think they meant to, they didn't know what they were doing, so crazy—Are you all right?" she asked again.

"Well, we nearly disappeared over the edge," Jack said, his voice shaking, not at all convinced whether Summer was telling the truth or if she was just covering up for her brother. "Maybe you guys threw them."

"Jack!" Ashley cried.

"Look at Ethan—he doesn't even care. If those rocks had hit us—"

"Jack, stop!" Steven ordered. "OK, that's it. Everyone back to the lodge. Now! Move!"

CHAPTER SEVEN

Standing outside the door to his parents' room, Jack listened to the soft hum of television voices inside and wondered for the hundredth time if what he was about to do was the right thing. Ashley, Summer, and Ethan were all resting for the big night ahead. Jack had waited until he'd heard Ethan's even breathing before slipping out and shutting the door slowly until it locked in place with a quiet click. He needed to talk to his parents. He needed to say out loud what he was thinking, why he was scared that Ethan might have sent the rocks down the mountain, and why he might try something again. But what if Jack was wrong? His dad certainly didn't believe Ethan had caused the rockfall. He'd lectured Jack and Ethan the whole way down the mountain trail.

"Ethan," his dad had said, "when I tell you that we need to stay together, I mean it. You can't go racing off ahead. Those teenagers could have kicked those rocks on your head too, you know. And Jack," he'd turned to Jack, his face set in a frown, "I know how scared you were, and when people are frightened they say things they regret. I'm sure you're sorry for accusing Ethan that way."

Jack had murmured an apology he didn't mean, which Ethan ignored. Now he was standing in front of a door, ready to stir the whole thing up again. Somewhere down the hall a vacuum cleaner whirred. A door slammed with a bang so loud it sounded like a gunshot, and outside a group of kids squealed.

A line from an old movie blinked through his mind like a neon sign: *Speak now, or forever hold your peace.* It was now or never. Taking in a breath, Jack gently tapped the wooden door with his knuckle. A moment later he was sitting on a queen-size bed, looking into the questioning eyes of his mother.

"You look pale, Jack. Are you feeling all right?"

"Yeah. I'm OK," Jack answered. He began to pull on the cuticle of his finger, unsure how to begin.

"I hear you had a pretty big scare today. When your dad told me you survived a rock slide I about had a heart attack. That's some pretty intense stuff." Cupping her hand around his neck, she said, "Is that why you're here? Did you want to talk about it?"

"Sort of. I—I want to tell you what I think really happened."

"You mean about the teenagers kicking the rocks down?"

Shaking his head, Jack tore the piece of skin so that a tiny dot of cherry-red blood began to appear. Looking up, he said, "I mean Ethan."

Afternoon light poured through the large window, illuminating a halo of curls around his mother's head as she faced him. In the backlight, her expression was hard to read, but Steven's feelings were clear enough; his head slowly shook from side to side, one shake, it seemed, for every word Jack spoke.

"Not this again. Jack, Summer said that it was an accident. Why would you even begin to think Ethan would try to harm us?"

"I don't know—lots of reasons. He doesn't like us. He says that all the time."

"It's difficult for him," his mother answered softly. "You know we talked about this already. We need to be patient."

"More important than that, son, is the fact that you're accusing Ethan on purely circumstantial evidence. Summer said other kids started that slide, and that's good enough for me." His voice took on a bit of an edge when he added, "And it should be good enough for you, too."

"Summer does whatever Ethan tells her to do," Jack protested. "If he told Summer to blame teenagers, then that's what she'd do."

"Is that all the proof you have? There's nothing else?" his mother asked.

"He kicked rocks at us in the cemetery—that's practically the same as starting a rock slide."

"I don't think it's anywhere near the same," his father answered.

"He ran away when you called him, Dad. He just blew you off and vanished up the mountain, and then suddenly, out of nowhere, comes a rock slide. I don't think that's normal, do you? And what about the way he's always whispering to Summer and acting like he wished we'd get out of his life." The last words came out in a rush, and then there was silence. His mother looked concerned whereas his father seemed almost irritated. Jack's stomach began to slide into his feet when his dad came and stood in front of him. There was no mistaking it now; his father was angry.

"I'm surprised at you, son. The whole idea of bringing other kids into this family—kids who haven't had all the breaks that you've had—was to teach you compassion. I thought you'd be able to walk around in someone else's shoes and see what it's like to be raised in a whole different way. But I guess it didn't work."

"Steven, he's just trying to tell us what he thinks," Olivia broke in.

"You're right, you're right." Taking a deep breath, Steven dropped into an overstuffed chair that had been pushed into a corner. "I'm sorry, Jack, maybe I'm getting a little too hot under the collar here. But if you're going to accuse someone, you've got to have more to go on than a bad feeling. This kind of stuff happened to me all the time when I was in foster care. It's hard to live under a cloud of suspicion just because you're different."

"Do you really think it was teenagers kicking down those rocks?" Jack asked, getting to his feet.

"Until I have proof otherwise, then I think we need to believe Ethan and Summer. I think we owe them that much." When his mother nodded in agreement, Jack turned to go. He'd come to his parents with his suspicions, and he'd been shot down. There was nothing more to do but hope they were right.

He used his key to slip back into his darkened room, crawling onto his bed as quietly as a cat. Even though jagged thoughts churned in his brain, when Jack hit the bed he slept like the dead—*dead,* as in what the Landons would have been if the rocks had landed on their heads. Even in the depth of his sleep, he heard the noises those rocks made bouncing off the canyon walls, like the collision of 16-pound balls against tenpins in a bowling alley. In a sweat, he awoke to find Ethan stretched out on his own bed, staring at the ceiling. Jack twisted to see the red digital numbers on the clock between their beds. 4:12. He'd slept for more than an hour.

At 4:16 the door to their room opened slowly. "You guys awake?" Olivia whispered. "We need to start out now if we're going to take part in the mustang capture tonight."

Jack rolled over and sat up on the bed. "Hey, Mom, I forgot to ask you—how'd it go with your lecture today?"

Olivia gave him a grin and a thumbs-up. "Great! I'll tell you all about it on our drive. Are you up, Ethan?"

"I'm awake."

"All right then, let's get moving. This mustang trapping is going to be quite an adventure!"

On the long drive toward the Chloride Canyon, Olivia chattered on and on about the seminar: "…so when your dad teased me yesterday about pinkeye in the deer population, he actually picked a good example of the different policies in the Park Service and the BLM. Mostly, though, I spoke about the condition of the deer population here in Zion National Park."

She turned in her seat to face the kids in the back. "Have you seen any deer since we've been here? They're kind of small and scraggly looking. We think it's because they've stopped migrating out of the park in the fall—they just stay here all year long. That means the herd's isolated, and getting too little fresh genetic material into the mix when they breed."

"That's cool, Mom," Jack told her. "So what are they going to do about the deer not getting any new genes?"

"New jeans?" Summer whispered, totally puzzled. "For the deer?"

"Not *those* kind of jeans," Ashley giggled. "Genes that are inside your cells—you know, that tell your body whether to make brown eyes or blue or white skin or red and all that kind of stuff."

"And if too many of the bad recessive genes hook together because they didn't get genetic variation, then you get problems," Jack explained, bewildering Summer even more.

"That's exactly what I was talking about at the seminar," Olivia said. "I suggested that the park people trap male deer from other areas and bring them in here to revitalize the herd, but it's national park policy to let nature take its course. So they're doing nothing." She raised her eyebrows in a "that's the way it is" expression.

His parents were being a lot like the Park Service, Jack mused. They were letting *human* nature take its course. The Landons could go on doing nothing and let Ethan keep secretly trying to hurt them—*if* that's what Ethan was doing. His dad's talk had succeeded in making Jack feel guilty about his suspicions, but that didn't make them go away.

Ethan sat slumped in his corner of the tailgate seat in the SUV. His fingers drummed the edges of his knees, where his jeans had worn thin. They looked like they could use a good washing—both the fingers and the jeans; he looked as punky as one of the scruffier deer in Zion. Well, Jack decided, he'd follow park policy and leave Ethan alone.

Acres of dried-up land reached into a horizon of low mountains and cloudless sky. All around him were barren, lifeless stretches of sand with occasional patches of sagebrush and blowing tumbleweed. It was hard to believe that Zion, with its color-drenched stone and brilliant green foliage, was only an hour's drive away. This land was open, flat, and lifeless. How could wild mustangs even survive out in this parched desert? Through the window, Jack watched the miles slip by.

Grinning mischievously, Ashley deliberately began to chant, "Are we there yet? Are we there yet?" since she knew how much it got on Jack's nerves.

"Stop it!" he hissed. "Don't be a dork."

"I wasn't asking you, I was asking Mom. Hey, Mom, are we there yet?"

Olivia was wrestling with the map. "I'm trying to figure out which road we're supposed to take," she answered. "I think we ought to be getting there pretty soon. And Ashley, I'll let you know when we get there. In other words, you don't have to ask again."

Funny, Jack thought—when they traveled, Steven usually did the driving, although Olivia was a perfectly good driver. Without ever talking about it, his parents seemed to divide their lives: His dad did the yard work, kept their car in good shape, and did most of the driving; his mother did the laundry, the food shopping, and packed the kids' lunches every day. Both of them liked to cook, so they took turns with that.

Jack and Ashley didn't have any boy/girl division in their chores; they both had to stack the dirty dishes in the dishwasher and take the clean dishes out, fold their own clothes, keep their personal junk out of the living room, and run the vacuum cleaner. He wondered about Ethan and Summer, whether they had to do chores in their grandmother's house on the reservation—or in what *used* to be their grandmother's house. The social worker said that starting now, their grandmother would spend the rest of her life in a nursing home.

Just to aggravate Jack, Ashley kept whispering, "Are we there yet? Are we there yet?" until he gave her an elbow in the ribs.

"Mo-om, Jack hit me," she whined, and then she started to laugh and said to Summer, "Just kidding. That's how we used to act when we were little and took long trips in the car."

Summer blinked uncertainly.

"Didn't you do that?" Ashley asked her. "You must have gone on long trips in a car with your brother, didn't you? Like, when you went to powwows?"

"Grandmother never had a car," Ethan answered. "So we never went anywhere, 'cause there was no bus, either. Just the school bus to junior high in Lander, outside the reservation. Summer doesn't ride the bus 'cause she's not in junior high yet."

"You mean your grandmother never left the reservation in her whole life?" Even though Jack hadn't been talking to Ethan, he couldn't help but blurt out the question. It seemed impossible that a person could live in the United States but never leave one tiny corner of it. Maybe it was because Jack and Ashley had been hauled around the country since they were old enough to walk.

"Not when she could decide for herself."

"What does that mean? Did she leave when she was younger?" Jack pressed.

Again Jack saw the flash of anger in Ethan's eyes as he answered, "When Grandmother was a little girl like Summer, white people came and took her to a boarding school. She was supposed to learn to be like a white person—she didn't want to, but they said she had to. They wouldn't let her talk in Shoshone, only in English. Once she forgot and said something in Shoshone, so they taped her mouth shut and made her scrub the whole big gym floor on her hands and knees to punish her. It took her all night."

That was the most words they'd ever heard all at once from Ethan, and it left the Landons in stunned silence. Is this what his dad meant when he said Jack should walk around in Ethan's shoes? As bad as all that sounded, Jack told himself, it still didn't give Ethan the right to roll rocks on their heads.

Steven answered, "Different times, different people,

Ethan. That would never happen today. Any school official who punished a kid that way would be fired. Or maybe even arrested."

Olivia added, "Lots of things have changed for the better since your grandmother was a little girl. For just one example, wild mustangs used to be rounded up, jammed into big trucks with horrible conditions, and shipped to slaughterhouses, where they were butchered for dog food. Today we protect the mustangs."

Ethan just turned his face to the window and peered out.

Dry and dusty, the rangeland that slid past their SUV now showed endless acres of yellowish brown grass, broken here and there by clumps of sagebrush and an occasional small tree. Behind the flat land, the mountains looked more like hills, cone-shaped brown hills dotted with junipers and piñon pines.

So this was the range that the Bureau of Land Management was sworn to protect. Fence posts made from stripped, narrow tree trunks held miles of barbed wire strung across the tops of the posts, and rows of telephone poles carried their own miles of electrical wires. To where? Jack couldn't see any houses. Not a single "home, home on the range." So who needed all that electricity?

Olivia rattled the map and said, "I think this is it. We're supposed to meet Art at this crossroad. Looks like we're right on time."

It was close to sundown—around seven in the evening. Orange and rose-colored clouds streaked the horizon.

"There he is," Steven said, "in that flatbed truck parked on the side of the road ahead of us." When they got closer, Art waved an arm out the window of the truck cab.

"Gus is with him, too," Ashley said. "But what's all that stuff in the back of the truck?"

"That's the corral they're going to set up at the water trap," Steven answered. He waved back at Art, who started his vehicle and motioned for Steven to follow him.

After a mile of dusty, unpaved road, Art stopped and Gus got out to open a gate. Once both vehicles had driven through, Gus closed the gate and got back in the truck.

"Worst thing you can do," Steven said, "is leave a gate open on rangeland. Sure as shootin', the cattle will find it, and they'll all get out and take a stroll along the highway."

"I haven't seen any cattle," Ashley said.

"They're around. They move a lot. It takes plenty of acreage to feed a cow."

They were no longer on any kind of road, but bumped along over the dirt and low brush, jarring the kids in the tailgate of the SUV. The sun was nearly gone, leaving only a faint smear of color along the horizon.

Finally Art came to a halt, and Steven stopped right behind him.

"Hi, Olivia, hi Steven, hi kids," Art said all in one breath. "Gotta hurry. Gotta set up these panels before it's too dark. Good thing there's so much manpower here—me and Gus, Steven and the two boys."

"Me too," Olivia said. "I may be short, but I'm pretty strong."

"And us too," Ashley said. "Me and Summer can help."

"Tell you what," Gus answered. "You girls see that stand of junipers over there?" He gestured to a clump of trees whose foliage looked almost black in the waning light. "That's where we're going to hide while we wait for the mustangs to come to the watering hole. Why don't you two go and clear the ground inside the trees so we can set there. We brought a couple little camp stools and some tarps."

"You want me to make a blind?" Summer asked.

"You really know how to make a blind?" Gus seemed surprised.

"Sure. I'm an Indian, you know."

"Then go right to it, honey," he told her. "There's a lot of us here, and we need plenty of cover to stay hid from those mustangs."

The men had begun to unload railed panels from the back of the truck, setting them upright around the small enclosed spring where the horses would come to drink. Each panel stood higher, even, than Steven's head, which was pretty high. The half dozen metal rails that made up the panels were unpainted to keep them from reflecting moonlight or even light from the stars, which would shine thick and bright overhead in that dark, isolated desert. Where one panel joined the next, the men slid bolt-like fasteners to hook them together.

Jack tried to help, but mostly he seemed to be in the way until Art told him, "See this here rope? One end'll be tied to the gate, but the gate's gotta stay open till the horses come inside—if we're lucky and they do come in. The rope's gonna stretch over to that bunch of junipers where we'll be hiding. When the horses get into the trap, we'll pull the rope and shut the gate on 'em."

"I get it," Jack said.

"So I'm gonna lay this rope down across the ground now, and you boys cover her up with dirt."

That didn't sound like a very exciting job, considering that the men got to set up panels around the spring. And since the trees stood about a hundred feet distant from the water trap, Jack and Ethan would have to do a lot of digging and covering up. As they got close to the blind, the last of the light faded, but not before Jack had noticed how skillfully Summer was weaving broken branches through the spaces between the trees. All of them would be well hidden.

By the time the full moon rose over Chloride Canyon, everything was in place.

"Now," Art said, "we wait. And we must stay *ab-so-lute-ly* quiet while we wait."

CHAPTER EIGHT

Jack had never before been in a situation like this. Eight people sat waiting in that blind made from juniper trees and broken branches, all of them in touching distance of one another, but no one spoke a single word. Not even a whisper. It had to be hard on Ashley, who was a nonstop talker, but she seemed content to lie on her back and watch the stars weave themselves into the bright, shining carpet of the Milky Way.

All through the first hour, Jack strained his ears to listen for whinnies in the distance, but he heard nothing except the rustling of the grass as the breeze played with it. Halfway into the second hour, he stopped looking at his watch, and his thoughts drifted. Drifted.... Maybe he was falling asleep. In his half-awake state he heard it—the same whinny he'd heard echoing off the cliffs the night before.

Now there were more whinnies—real ones, not

dream ones. A sense of movement beside him pulled him into wakefulness. Even in the dark, he could tell that the other people waiting with him had become tense. The mustangs were coming to drink!

They were graceful shadows in the moonlight, flowing leisurely across the range, knowing where they were headed. An even dozen of them—Jack could count them, although he couldn't tell their colors because all he could see were silhouettes.

They came closer, whinnying and nickering constantly as though holding a horse conversation of vital importance. Now Jack could see that three of them were white, the rest darker in color. The white ones kept close to the others, actually touching their noses to the darker horses' flanks. One white mustang laid its head on the rump of the horse in front of it. When the herd stopped abruptly, the white mustangs whinnied long and loudly, as though questioning what the problem might be.

The herd had noticed the panels erected around the spring. Circling cautiously outside the trap, they snorted and sniffed, examining this new contraption that stood between them and their nightly drink. The white horses shuffled impatiently, shaking their heads so that their black manes tossed.

Earlier, while the Landons and the others had waited for the mustangs to arrive, time had dragged. Now Jack didn't even think about checking his watch; his eyes stayed riveted on the restless, nervous herd. The mustangs knew that their accustomed source of water lay very near, beyond those metal rails, but this strange barrier puzzled them.

There was a way to reach the water—they'd figured that out, too. The gate stood wide open, inviting them inside. Yet they hesitated, because something so strange and unknown might be a threat. One heavily muscled dark brown stud, the obvious leader of the herd, stamped the ground fretfully. Wary, with his head lowered and his legs spread wide, he stuck his nose inside the gate, then backed up quickly and snorted. The other mustangs continued to mill around. Again, the dark mustang nosed past the gate; this time he took a few steps forward. Nothing happened. He took a few more steps.

The people crouched inside the blind held their breath. The night was still, except for a slight rustling in the juniper trees as the breeze drifted among the branches. Now the dominant stud approached the water. Lowering his head, he began to drink, but he raised his head frequently to look around.

Outside the gate, the other horses nickered rest-lessly. Another darker-colored horse moved toward the water; behind it, nose against flank, came one of the white horses. A fourth mustang, smaller and not quite white, followed. Jack imagined Art's hand reaching for the rope that would swing the gate shut and trap the animals inside the fence. Soon, now....

Suddenly Summer cried out, "Ethan, they're ghost horses! Don't let the ghost horses get trapped!"

Almost instantly Ethan was on his feet, breaking through the shrubbery of the blind. Waving a branch in his hand, he yelled, "Hi yuh! Get out of here! Run!"

Pandemonium broke loose. Like shadows exploding in the moonlight, the mustangs scattered every which way. The four horses inside the metal-rail trap crashed against the railings, and in their panic to get out, knocked over two of the panels. Art and Gus rushed out from the blind to try to keep the structure from toppling over; Steven hurried after them to help.

The whinnying crescendoed as all the dark-colored horses galloped away, flank to flank, while three white horses ran in tight, panicky circles, their heads high, their ears laid back. One, a white stallion, broke away from the other horses and raced toward the juniper blind, where Olivia, Jack, Ashley, and Summer were still half hidden.

"Look at that horse!" Jack yelled.

The white stallion ran forward a little way, reared up, turned, and ran again as though unsure which direction to take. Then he turned once more toward the blind and began to gallop.

"It's coming to get us!" Summer screamed.

"It won't—" Olivia began, but before she could get out any more words the stallion had crashed into the trees right in front of them. He screamed and twisted, rearing up and slashing at the sky with his front hoofs while the kids dove out of the way. In her fright, Ashley tripped over a tree root. She fell to the ground just beneath the stallion's flailing hooves.

Jack didn't think; he reacted. Grabbing Ashley's feet, he yanked her out of the way just as the stallion's front hoofs hit the ground, so close to her head that her hair got caught beneath one forefoot. Her shrieks merged with the screams of the stallion into one shrill cry of terror. As the mustang danced, Jack gave a mighty tug to pull Ashley clear just before the horse crashed down again. Whinnying and bleeding from the places where broken branches had torn his hide, the stallion turned and burst out of the blind. He circled to reach the rest of the herd, then galloped off with them into the night.

Ashley was so terrified that for once she couldn't talk at all. Neither could Olivia, who held her daughter tightly in her arms, her head buried against Ashley's for a long moment before she looked up at her son.

"Jack," she began, "you—Ashley—" She couldn't go on.

"It's OK," Jack answered, patting his mother's arm. "Ashley isn't hurt."

Steven had started running toward them when he saw the stallion closing in on the blind, but because of the shadowy darkness of the juniper trees, he'd been unable to tell the seriousness of the situation. "What happened?" he cried when he reached them.

Olivia could only answer, "Thankfully we're all safe."
Art and Gus, who'd righted the panels around the water
trap, now came stomping back toward the kids.

"What the crud did you two think you were doing?"
Art demanded loudly, standing in front of Ethan and
Summer, his hands on his hips.

"Yeah, Ethan," Jack began, but his father caught his
eye and shook his head.

Summer was crying; more than crying—she was
sobbing. Ethan stood with his shoulders hunched,
his eyes squeezed shut and his head lowered, as if
waiting for a beating to begin.

Stepping between Art and Ethan, Steven said, "I'll
deal with them. I'm really sorry about what happened."

"Well," Gus said, "there's still a chance the mustangs
will come back. They gotta drink! Wild horses need
about ten to twenty gallons a day. Those mustangs won't
want to go through the whole night without water."

"Will you stay here?" Olivia asked, her voice so
strained Jack wouldn't have recognized it if he hadn't
seen her speak.

"Yeah, me and Art. We'll wait through the night.
Maybe we'll get lucky, and they'll come back."

Firmly grasping Ethan and Summer by the arms,
Steven led them across the hundred yards of brush
to where he'd hidden the SUV behind a clump of
juniper trees. Olivia followed with Jack and Ashley

but lagged behind so she could talk to them without being overheard.

"Jack, you saved your sister's life," she said, and had to stop so she could hug him. "Do you realize what you did? She could have been killed if it hadn't been for you."

Suddenly Jack felt wild elation. He *had* saved Ashley! Never before in his life had he done anything like it. A few times they'd been in tight scrapes together when he'd probably kept Ashley from harm, but this was the closest they'd come to an actual threat of death. Those flailing hoofs would have crushed her skull. He felt his chest swelling as though his lungs had doubled. He'd done it!

"I just don't understand what was wrong with that stallion," Olivia was saying. "In all my years of being a vet, I've never seen a horse behave like that. He ran straight into the trees—not *between* them, but *against* the trees, like he could pass right through them without harm, as though he were invisible."

"Ghost horse," Ashley said, and shuddered.

Pursing her lips, Olivia shook her head. "No, he was very real. I saw him, I heard him, I smelled him, and he nearly trampled you. He was no ghost."

Ahead of them, Steven was talking sternly to Summer and Ethan but was focusing more intently on Ethan. Jack wished he could hear what his father was saying. He hoped Steven was chewing Ethan out, telling him how crazy he'd acted and how awful he was to put Ashley's life in danger. He watched his father waving his arms as he spoke, as though he were conducting music instead of having a conversation.

When they reached the SUV, Olivia said, "Jack, you ride up front with your father. I want to sit in the backseat with Ashley." Without a word, Ethan and Summer climbed into the tailgate and disappeared into its shadows. Jack was really glad they'd rented an SUV with three rows of seats; right then he wanted to be alone with his dad. Maybe Steven would thank him for saving Ashley's life. It would be the two Landon men, just the way it was going to be tomorrow when they hiked The Narrows together.

No one spoke as the SUV bumped along across the tufts of grass, occasionally zigzagging around sagebrush. Jack pulled down the visor so he could look into the mirror and see what was going on in back of him. Ashley was sprawled out across the backseat, her head in her mother's lap as Olivia stroked her hair. Summer and Ethan were whispering together in the tailgate, with Ethan's arm draped awkwardly across his sister's shoulders.

Jack decided to get the ball rolling. "I hope Art and Gus aren't too mad," Jack said quietly to his father. "I couldn't believe Ethan wrecked their trap. What a total jerk he is."

"Who?"

"Ethan! He ruined everything tonight, and he could have killed Ashley."

"I don't know about that."

"Dad, that stallion almost cracked Ashley's head like a walnut. If I hadn't pulled her out of there, well, Mom says I saved Ashley's life!"

"You were very brave, son."

Jack twisted in his seat so that he could get a better look at his father. Steven's strong hands gripped the steering wheel hard, and in the faint light from the dashboard, Jack could see a stubble of blond hair on his father's chin. This discussion wasn't going the way Jack had planned, but he didn't know what to say to get the conversation on track. It almost seemed as though his dad was on Ethan's side. But that was impossible. If Jack had done half of what Ethan did, Jack would have been grounded for a month. Maybe the whole year.

"So—did you yell at Ethan?"

"We had a talk. But I really think that's between Ethan and me." He stole a quick glance at Jack. "OK?"

"Fine," Jack said woodenly. The SUV's headlights cut through the darkness, and overhead the stars seemed to hang heavy in the night sky. Disappointment gnawed at his insides like tiny teeth. He was sure his dad was taking Ethan's side.

"You all right, Jack?" Steven asked softly.

Jack shrugged.

"Come on, what's up?"

"Dad, don't you think this whole thing is really strange? I mean, first you almost get crushed by Hal, then there's a bunch of rocks that almost crash down on our heads, and now Ashley almost gets squashed by a wild mustang."

"So?"

"So I think it's weird that ever since we've been around the Ingawanups, we've had bad luck."

"I don't believe in luck, Jack. Other than the kind you make for yourself."

"Right," Jack said, his voice rising. "Maybe Ethan has done some of this on purpose. Maybe he planned to yell at the horses to get them to stampede. Maybe it really was Ethan who sent the rocks down the mountain at Angels Landing. Dad, I think—I think we should send Ethan back."

Steven was silent for so long that Jack thought he wasn't going to answer. Then, out of nowhere, he said to Jack, "I picked up a newspaper this afternoon in the lobby of the lodge. There was an article in it about a herd of mustangs that ranged not too far away from here, on BLM land about a hundred miles to the east."

What did this have to do with Ethan? Jack waited for his dad to continue. After a minute he asked, "What about them?"

"There were 27 horses in that herd," Steven said. "They'd always watered at the same place, at a spring.

But because the weather this past summer was pretty hot and dry, the spring dried up."

Again Jack had to wait until Steven continued, "There was another water source about six miles away, and six miles is nothing to horses. But these mustangs had always watered at the same spring, and when the spring dried up, the herd just stayed put. Stayed there and waited. And waited."

Jack was beginning to wonder about the point of all this. "So what happened?" he asked.

"They got weaker and weaker until they died of dehydration."

"All of them?" Jack asked, startled. "All 27?"

"Most of them. Four lived. The BLM folks are nursing them back to health, and when they're well enough, they'll be put up for adoption."

Jack felt a wrenching in his gut because the story was so awful. Why was his dad telling him this?

"If they'd only gone a little farther," Steven said, "they'd have found all the water they needed. But they wouldn't look over the next mountain. They were stubborn. Or foolish. They stayed with what they were used to."

Now Jack got it. Steven was talking about Summer and Ethan, who'd spent all their lives in the same place and wouldn't adjust to new ways. Maybe they couldn't see what a great opportunity they had in living with the Landons.

"Do you see what I'm getting at, Jack?" Steven asked him.

"Yeah, Dad, I do."

"Well then, how about if you quit being so stubborn. It's time for you to look over the next mountain and figure out what's there when you're dealing with Ethan. You might discover something new and valuable."

"Me?" Jack squeaked. "You're talking about *me?*"

"Yes, you. Think about it, son. That's all I wanted to say."

CHAPTER NINE

It's time to get up, Jack. We need to get moving—The Narrows awaits."

Steven's rumbling voice, and then the click of the door as he went back into his own room, pulled Jack out of his sleep. The red numbers on the digital clock blinked 8:00. This is what he'd been waiting for, had been planning for ever since he'd heard his family would be going to Zion. Now it was finally happening. He knew it would be a chance to take the finest photographs of his life. Stretching, Jack sat up and looked over at Ethan's bed. It was empty. Confused, Jack whirled around until he saw Ethan, a dark shape in a corner chair, shadowed by the thick, closed drapes. He was staring at Jack.

"Ethan, what are you doing?" he asked, too groggy to remember they hadn't spoken since before the run-in with the wild mustang. "Why are you sitting there?"

"Do you believe it?" Ethan's voice sounded cold and flinty.

"Believe what? What are you talking about?"

For a moment Ethan waited, silent. Hidden in half-light, his face had become shadow within shadow, making it impossible to read. Reaching over and flicking on the light, Jack turned back to face his adversary. Somehow Ethan had managed to get dressed without waking Jack; his hair hung wild against his white T-shirt, and his arms were crossed tight. "I heard what you said last night. To your dad. You said I tried to hurt Ashley. Do you believe it?" His eyebrows made dark arches over his eyes.

Jack's mind suddenly grew clear as he remembered last night. So Ethan had been listening. He felt a flash of embarrassment that he quickly quenched. Ethan had been eavesdropping on a private conversation. If he didn't like what he'd heard, well, that was his fault. "Yeah," Jack answered aggressively. "Yeah, I'm saying you're up to something."

"You think I would kick rocks on your head? You think I would hurt Ashley on purpose? Your father doesn't believe I would do that."

"My dad was an orphan, so he can't believe any foster kid can be bad. You have him fooled. Not me."

Ethan was on his feet, shoulders squared, his fists in tight balls. Slowly, he walked over to Jack, his muscles bulging and dark eyes flashing. "Take it back."

"No way!"

"I said—" Ethan gave Jack a hard push—"take it back! You think you know everything, but you don't know nothin' about our lives. You're just like the white people who hurt my grandmother!"

"Don't blame me for stuff that happened before I was even born. *You're* the one who's trying to hurt *us!*"

"If I was going to hurt you, you'd know it!" Ethan gave Jack another shove, this time knocking him off balance. In a flash, Jack was on top of Ethan, and the two of them were suddenly tangled up, punching each other and the air as hard as they could. Ethan's knuckle grazed Jack's front tooth, and Jack tasted blood in his mouth. His own punch landed under Ethan's eye. Jack could hear the sound of fist on skin and the jar of the punch that raced all the way up into his shoulder socket. Suddenly the door flew open and his father was yanking them apart, shouting for each one of them to stop this nonsense, while his mother cried, "Jack, what do you think you're doing?"

"Me! What about Ethan?" Jack was so mad, he felt the words jam one on top of the other. "Why aren't you yelling at him?"

"Because you're our son. You know our rules about fighting!"

"But Ethan's the one who started it—"

His father barked, "Enough!" so loud that the rest of the sentence withered in Jack's mouth. Ethan stood with his head bowed. Silence filled the room, a cold silence punctuated only by Jack's and Ethan's heavy breathing. All Jack wanted to do now was to pack his backpack and get away from Ethan. When his father finally spoke, the words were slow, deliberate.

"You two have been at odds since we picked up Ethan at Wind River. It's got to stop. The only way I know to do that is by making you spend time together. You're two great kids. If you get to know each other, you'll find that out."

Silence.

"Ethan, today Jack and I are going hiking in The Narrows as planned. It's going to be quite an experience—"

Suddenly, all the air and light seemed to disappear out of the room as a chill spread from Jack's chest all the way through his body. His father was going to invite Ethan along. On *his* trip! "No—Dad—you can't—"

"Jack, be quiet. I'm not talking to you. Ethan, would you like to join us?"

With his eyes still glued to the floor, Ethan shook his head no.

"Let me rephrase. Ethan, you are going to accompany Jack and me on a marvelous hike into the Zion Narrows. You two are going to work this out, and I'm going to keep you together until you do. This can be as hard or as easy as you'd like it to be. Understand?"

"Yes," Ethan said softly.

"Jack?"

Jack couldn't trust himself to speak. Finally, he nodded.

"Good. Then we all understand one another. Now we're going down to eat in the dining room, and then I want the two of you to come into my room to pack. You *will* be civil to each other. You *will* be respectful. Or you *will*"—Steven narrowed his eyes as he looked from one to the other—"be very sorry!"

At breakfast, Olivia told them, "I got a phone call early this morning from Art. Just a little before dawn, he and Gus were able to trap some mustangs at the water hole. One was the white stallion who ran into us last night, another is a mature white mare, plus they caught a couple of others from the herd."

Jack just nodded. He had problems of his own to worry about.

"Summer and Ashley and I are going to drive there this morning to take a look at the mustangs he trapped."

His hopes rising, Jack said, "So Ethan can go with you."

"Jack!" his father warned, pointing a fork in Jack's direction. "You know what the plan is. End of discussion. Now finish your scrambled eggs. You'll need a good meal under your belt for our hike."

On the way upstairs after breakfast, Steven told Jack, "I want you to come into my room. We have about an hour's work before we can leave."

"What kind of work?" Jack asked.

"We're going to hike the Zion Narrows, remember? That means we'll be wading through the Virgin River for a couple of miles. The water won't be all that deep, but there are holes and drop-offs where it'll come up as high as your chest. We need to seal everything in plastic freezer bags to keep our stuff from getting soaked."

Jack was surprised when he saw all the things Steven had spread out on his bed: In addition to the freezer bags, there were a bunch of wooden matches stuck into a film canister; a pocket knife; three pairs of thick socks; three sweatshirts; a box of Band-Aids; half a dozen granola bars; six one-pint bottles of water; six wrapped sandwiches, with a bunch of little plastic packs of ketchup and mustard that Steven must have bought at the coffee shop; plus a trio of four-inch-diameter, M&M-dotted sugar cookies, individually packaged in plastic wrappers that said "Grandma's Best."

"Do we have to carry all that?" Jack asked. "I thought we were only going for half a day. That's enough stuff for a week!"

"You're a Boy Scout. You ought to know you need to 'be prepared,'" Steven answered. "This is no wimpy hike we're going on. The Narrows can be difficult, not to mention potentially dangerous. Now go call Ethan, and we'll pack this stuff into our backpacks."

As usual, Ethan found something to object to. "You

want me to carry *that* backpack?" he protested. "It's purple! It's for a girl."

"You're right, it's Ashley's," Steven answered.

"No way! I ain't gonna—" Ethan began.

Jack could tell his dad was in a no-fooling-around mode when he said, "Why? Because it has pink straps? It won't kill you to carry it."

"It's the only other backpack we have," Jack snapped. "If you don't like it, tough. You can always stay here."

"Maybe I will!"

"Jack, no arguing, remember? Ethan, as far as using Ashley's backpack—yes, you're gonna." Softening a little, Steven said, "Listen, Ethan, the worst thing that could happen would be for someone to see you carrying that girly backpack and then go back to the Wind River Reservation and tell it to all the guys you hang out with. So how many people do you think you'll run across today who will recognize you and squeal on you back at the reservation?"

"None," Ethan answered grudgingly.

"Correct. So start packing. And Jack, double-seal your camera."

It was past 10:00 by the time they'd hiked to the top of the paved trail that ended at The Narrows. Steven paused before a large wooden sign that read: "ALL NARROW CANYONS ARE POTENTIALLY HAZARDOUS. FLASH FLOODS, COLD WATER, AND

STRONG CURRENTS PRESENT REAL DANGERS THAT CAN BE LIFE-THREATENING. YOUR SAFETY DEPENDS ON YOUR OWN GOOD JUDGMENT, ADEQUATE PREPARATION, AND CONSTANT ATTENTION. BY ENTERING A NARROW CANYON, YOU ARE ASSUMING A RISK."

For a long moment, Steven stayed silent. Then he said, "Well, I think we're prepared, and I hope I'm using good judgment taking you kids on this hike. But we'll have to be really careful." He pointed to a pile of sticks about five feet long and two fingers thick stacked together on the ground. "OK, grab one," he said.

"What are they?" Jack asked.

"Walking sticks. A guy at the lodge told me not to bother buying any because people leave them here when they've finished hiking The Narrows. We borrow them, use them, and return them to this place for the next hikers."

"Why do we need to carry sticks?" Ethan wanted to know.

"To keep our balance. The river bottom is slippery. The sticks are like having a third leg."

From that point on there was no more paved trail or path of any kind—they waded right into the river. All three of them wore tennis shoes, shorts, and T-shirts and carried backpacks—Ethan still glowering because his was purple.

The Narrows was narrow, for sure. The high, red

slickrock walls were so close together that only a thin blue strip of sky could be seen overhead. Wading became tricky; their tennis shoes slipped on the rocks in the riverbed, which made their ankles turn a lot. Jack wished he'd worn his hiking boots, even though it would have meant getting them soaked. Lacing them high would have guarded his ankles. He knew why he'd had to wear sneakers, and why Steven was wearing his, too—it was because Ethan didn't have any hiking boots. In Steven's mind, it wouldn't have been fair for Jack and Steven to be better equipped than Ethan. Jack had been about to argue about wearing his boots when his mother put her hand on his shoulder. Her soft eyes had searched his as she said, "Jack, your father and I are trying to smooth out the troubles between you and Ethan. I'm asking you to please try. Please?"

So Jack was trying to be halfway civil. It was more for himself, really, since he couldn't let Ethan ruin this day. Not one this important.

Only a hundred yards from the end of the paved trail, the water level had risen from ankle deep to hip deep—at least for Steven. Since the boys weren't as tall, the water reached all the way to their ribs before the river became shallower again. The current wasn't strong enough to bother them, but they definitely felt it pushing against their legs. And the water felt cold.

Each step stirred up sand and gravel from the river bottom; Jack's shoes were beginning to fill with the stuff.

He really wanted to sit down and empty the sand out of his shoes, but there was no place close by to sit. No riverbank, no pile of rocks to climb on, only sheer, slick canyon walls. Both Jack and his dad had slung their cameras on straps around their necks, and they stopped often to take pictures—straight up!

"Wow, Dad, did you get that shot? It's great!" Jack tried to sound extra enthusiastic since Ethan didn't have a camera, and he was still mad enough to try to needle Ethan wherever he could. Craning back, Jack hit the button on his camera again and again. The view was nothing short of incredible.

"Try to frame the sky with the walls," his father instructed. Jack bent backward even farther; he liked the sensation of standing still in the river and slowly, slowly raising his gaze, from the base of the sheer-walled, orange-colored gorge—up and up and up even higher—till his eyes reached the very top of the cliffs. The sight was dizzying. It made him feel like he was going to topple over backward.

Two more hours would have to pass before the sun would stand directly over them, warm enough to dry them partway. Only at midday would they be able to see the sun itself—the rest of the time it was hidden by the high, shadowed, nearly vertical canyon walls. The water was about 60 degrees—real chilly—and in his wet clothes Jack was beginning to feel uncomfortable. To get a chance to rest, he called out, "Dad, did you know your backpack strap isn't fastened around your chest? Wait up for a minute, and I'll fix it for you."

Steven answered, "I left it unfastened on purpose. If I step into a deep hole, like up to my neck, the pack'll float so the water won't rush into it as much. If I had it strapped around me, it'd get dunked. Whoa! Like now!" Steven yelled. Not only had he stepped into a hole, he'd tripped into it face first. But even as he fell, he threw up his arms, holding the camera high, managing to keep it from getting wet. The fall jolted his hiking stick out of his hand. It drifted slowly down river.

Ethan started to laugh—the first time Jack had ever heard Ethan Ingawanup laughing out loud. "Yaaah!" Steven yelled, floundering as he hauled himself to his feet. "Hey, grab my stick! It's coming right at you. See it?" Gesturing toward the stick made him veer off balance, and he fell once more into the water, this time bottom first, with his backpack floating behind him. Only his head, and his arm holding up the camera, stuck up above the water's surface. He looked like a submerged Statue of Liberty.

Ethan was practically bent over laughing, and Jack felt irritation surge through him. What right did Ethan have to mock Jack's father, especially after the way Steven was always taking Ethan's side against Jack, always standing up for him, always telling everyone to be so nice to poor little underprivileged Ethan.

"Knock it off!" Jack snarled.

"Hey, it's just as much your fault as mine," Ethan answered, still snorting with hilarity. "That's why it's so funny. You made it happen."

"My fault? I wasn't even near him!"

"You did the Ghost Dance." Ethan's mirth was starting to subside. "It's really working."

"Ghost Dance? What are you talking about?"

"Sure," Ethan answered, now perfectly serious. "Think about all those creepy things that have been happening to your family. Not like your father slipping in the river right now—that's nothing. But the rocks falling yesterday, and the mustang nearly stomping your sister last night. You said it was my fault. Maybe you're right. But you helped."

"You're crazy!"

Steven had waded up to them now. He'd heard what Ethan was saying, and asked him, "You think the Ghost Dance caused those accidents?"

"Do *I* think?" Ethan didn't answer that, but he said, "The Shoshone used to believe in it—a hundred years ago. Maybe some still do. They danced the Ghost Dance to make white people go away. What's so great about it right now is"—Ethan began to laugh again, but it was not a pleasant sound as he pointed a finger at Jack— "like, what cracks me up is that Jack and Ashley danced the Ghost Dance, too, and it's supposed to get rid of white people. You danced to get rid of yourselves."

Steven said nothing, but his jaw began to work, and his fist clenched slightly. He just stared at Ethan, who stared right back, his stone-person expression in place again. Finally Steven said, "The trail map shows a sand-bar around the bend from here. I think it's a good time for us to stop and eat."

So Steven was going to let it go. Again. Jack mulled it over, deciding that the superstition about the Ghost Dance wasn't what bothered him—he didn't believe in stuff like that. He didn't think Ethan did, either, since Ethan wouldn't answer either yes or no when Steven asked him straight out.

It was Ethan's attitude that made Jack burn. That kid had the biggest and baddest attitude Jack had ever come across. Jack was ready to spit out an insult, but Steven was giving him a don't-make–a-big-deal-out-of-this look, so Jack had to hold it in. One more item to add to the long rap sheet of offenses by Ethan Ingawanup.

Rocks aren't the most comfortable things to sit on, but the air was warm, the sandwiches tasted great, and no one else was around. Just three guys—two blond, one Native American. Two fatherless, one lucky enough to have a father who cared so much, both about his own son and about all fatherless children, no matter what punky jerks they turned out to be.

Above them, the rock walls were streaked with dark zebra stripes from minerals that had leached out of the surface over thousands of years. Since no one was talking—just chewing—it was quiet enough to hear the splashing of the Virgin River as it veered around the rocks that studded its bed, and the faint twitter of birds on the cliffs so high overhead, and another sound much fainter, so far away that Jack wasn't even sure he'd heard it. Thunder, maybe, but far, far in the distance. It didn't repeat, so he didn't mention it to his father.

"When you guys are finished," Steven said, "we'll hike up past Orderville Canyon. The water gets deeper there, and the walls get really close together, so it might be tricky to take pictures. I'm going to put away my camera for now." He began sealing his dry bag around his camera and flash attachment.

Heading north, they trekked back into the river.

Steven had been correct—just as they passed Orderville Canyon, which veered off to their right, the water did get deeper, and the current pushed harder against Jack's legs. "Ow!" he yelled.

"What's wrong?" his dad asked from where he was wading behind the two boys.

"A stick hit me on the leg. Here comes another one." Jack managed to step out of the way of the second stick borne along on the current. But a third one slammed into his shin. "Hey, that hurts! Where are all these sticks coming from?"

"OK, stop, both of you," Steven ordered. He peered intently into the flowing water, which was no longer as clear as it had been earlier. It looked a little muddy. Bits of sticks and other debris floated toward them. Just then, Jack heard the thunder again. This time there was no mistaking it, although it still sounded far away, and the sky overhead remained blue and cloudless.

"That's thunder!" Steven told them, his voice sharp as he searched the sky intently. This time it was Ethan who gave a sharp cry. "Hey! A big stick just hit me!"

The color seemed to suddenly drain from Steven's face. "Turn around! Quick!" he barked.

"Why—" Jack began, but Steven cut him off with, "We gotta get out of here! Fast!"

CHAPTER TEN

What's happening?" Jack yelled. The current was growing stronger.

"Flash flood," Steven shouted above the rushing sound of water.

Jack felt his eyes widen with fear; he knew what a flash flood meant. People died in flash floods. All the time. "But—it's not even raining!" Jack sputtered. "How—"

"It rained upriver. Don't talk—move your feet! Both of you get in front of me. Go!"

There was no way to run in water that flowed knee high. In an unbelievably short time it came all the way up to their hips. They were moving in the same direction as the current, but as the flow grew swifter and stronger, they had to fight to keep from being knocked off their feet and swept downriver. The deeper the river, the more turbulent it became. Its waters roiled with churned-up mud and sand that scoured the backs of their legs.

"Is this as deep as it will get? 'cause I can handle this," Ethan yelled.

Jack jerked his head upstream and hollered, "It's just the beginning. Look for a ledge, a branch—anything to hold on to!"

Without saying a word, Ethan nodded. Jack kept whipping around to see his father, and Steven kept looking back to discover what might be coming. He tried to deflect the branches and debris swept forward by the river, to keep it from hitting the boys, but it was like trying to stop a bombardment of gnats—swat a few, and the rest kept closing in. "Find a ledge!" he kept yelling.

Jack scanned the sheer rock walls and saw nothing but rose-colored sandstone as smooth as tile. Nowhere to escape. Nothing to grab. It became harder and harder to stay upright.

"Dad—the water's getting higher!"

"A stone just smacked my leg!" Ethan bellowed. "Man, that hurt!"

"There's a ledge!" Steven cried. "Move!" He had to shout because the torrent was making so much noise—branches cracking, rocks rolling and pounding against each other in that same bowling-alley racket the rocks had made tumbling down the mountain. And once again, the sound of thunder, although it was still far away.

"Get to the ledge," Steven kept yelling. "Hurry! The crest can come any second!"

The crest. Jack knew that when it hit, anything in its path would be swept away in a wall of water churning with rocks and tree limbs. Anyone caught in it could drown—or get battered to death. Don't think—just move! he commanded himself. Was it the cold water—or fear—that filled his insides with ice?

In less than a minute they'd reached the rock ledge that jutted out over the water, like a life raft in an ocean. Jack felt a surge of hope; if they could climb on it, they'd be safe. Ethan shoved ahead of him, Steven trailed after. Only a few feet to go.

"Come on, get up!" Steven ordered, grabbing Ethan and lifting him. Ethan clutched the ledge and pulled himself up the rest of the way. "Hurry, Jack," Steven panted.

"Dad—what about you?"

Jack felt his father's strong arms raise him out of the water. "Pull," Steven yelled to Ethan. From above, Ethan reached down to take Jack's hand, yanking him up.

Gripping the ledge with his hands, Steven was ready to boost himself up when a sudden breeze swept over them, followed by the thunderous roar of debris-filled water bursting in their direction. Steven shouted, "Move back! Here comes the crest!"

"Dad!" Jack screamed, but the words were sucked back into his mouth as the roar filled his ears and pounded through his head. Steven hung on while the crest of the flash flood washed past him, battering him with mud and water. Sputtering, he came up for air while Jack reached down to grab his father's hands. Just then a large cedar branch hit the edge of the rock outcropping. It ricocheted upward. The splintery bottom of the branch slashed Steven across his fingers and the top flew up to smack Jack at the base of his skull.

Everything went dark. Jack could hear sounds. Someone was shouting, "Hold him," and he felt himself grabbed around the chest. With tremendous effort he opened his eyes to see his father's bleeding fingers slip from the edge of the rocks. "Take care of Jack," Steven seemed to be shouting, and then he was gone. Jack wanted to say something to his father, something important, wanted to see if he was still there, but golden lights kept flashing through the blackness in front of his eyes, blurring all that mattered.

He felt himself laid roughly onto his back. Everything whirled around in his head like the blades of a giant mixer—the roar of rushing water, the coldness of the rock beneath him, Ethan bending over him. Slowly, words began to form inside him; to Ethan, he said, "Tell my dad—"

Ethan just shook his head.

"Gone?"

"He'll be OK." But the look on Ethan's face contradicted him.

"Dad—I've got to—help him!" Jack tried to roll himself off the ledge, but Ethan's grip was as tight as a vise.

"He's OK. He had this big branch that he was holding onto, and he just floated away like he caught some raft or something. Don't worry about your dad."

"You're lying," Jack said weakly, and then he had to roll over again because he was throwing up.

A huge boulder smacked into the wall with an impact that sounded like a thunderclap, causing Jack to jerk up. "My head—" he groaned. He could feel the blood pound through his skull with every beat of his heart. He'd never felt pain like this before. Nothing else existed except his head and the pain that shot through him and the nausea and the cold of the rock that was beginning to numb his skin.

"Hey, I told you to quit moving. You've got to lie still. You got yourself hit. Let me see how bad. I'm going to turn your head, just a little."

Sparks of pain shot through Jack's skull as Ethan, tried to gently lift him. Crying out, he saw whirls of light explode in front of his eyes.

"Sorry, Jack. I won't do that again."

"Bad?" Jack asked. He couldn't believe how hard it was to move his lips. Things inside his head were slowing down, as though his brain were dragging though quicksand.

"I don't know. You're bleeding. There's a cut. Right here." Ethan pointed to the base of his own skull.

"Cut?" Why would he have a cut? Jack tried to remember, but thoughts were dropping away from him like leaves in a storm. They kept flying off, and he couldn't follow them.

Ethan's long hair stuck against his forehead and his neck, and his T-shirt plastered his body. "I gotta think," he kept telling Jack. "Gotta think what to do."

The words made no sense. Jack felt cold, so cold. Shivers wrenched his body, shaking his teeth. When he looked up, he saw two Ethans rummaging through Jack's backpack, but sometimes they melted together into one Ethan, and then there were two of them again, tearing open a large plastic bag to pull out a sweatshirt. "I'm afraid to lift you," Ethan said, spreading the shirt on top of Jack. "Once I got whacked on the head like that playing football, and they said I had to lie still but not go to sleep."

"But I'm sleepy," Jack murmured drowsily.

"No, don't!" Squatting beside him, Ethan said, "We'll talk. I'll say something, and you say something back."

"Ghost Dance," Jack murmured weakly, and with tremendous effort he was able to speak the rest of the words. "It made another white man go away. My dad." A deep sadness filled his chest, but he could no longer remember what he felt so sad about.

Protests began to pour out of Ethan's mouth the way the water was pouring down the canyon. "No!" he shouted. "The stuff about the Ghost Dance getting rid of white people—that's all garbage. Listen, you know why I said we'd dance the Ghost Dance? There's another part to it. It was supposed to bring dead Indians back to life. The Shoshone really believed in that when they danced it a hundred years ago."

Jack frowned, having trouble understanding what Ethan was saying. When he squinted, Ethan was still double. Both Ethans looked like they were crying.

"I didn't believe any of it—I knew it was all garbage—but I kept wishing the magic would work just once to bring back my mother and father. I was five when they died. I hardly remember them."

Jack's lips tried to shape the words, but his lips wouldn't twist right. "Did—" he managed to say.

"Did it work? Maybe."

Jack wanted to bend his fingers. He couldn't—they were too cold.

"These last two nights, my parents came to me in dreams. They told me I should quit being so mad. But you kept making me mad, Jack." Ethan pulled a dry sweatshirt out of his own pack and spread it across Jack's legs. "Look, as soon as the water goes down, I'll get you out of here. Don't go to sleep! Jack—I want you to say something. Keep talking at me, man. Say a word. Any word."

"Aperture," Jack mumbled.

"What's that supposed to mean?"

Jack couldn't think what it meant—it was the

only word that had stumbled into his mind. It had something to do with cameras, maybe. The spinning of his brain was so violent, and the back of his skull hurt so much that each syllable dug into him like a dentist's drill.

The two Ethans began to rub Jack's arms, hard. "Listen, here's my word. Fort Washakie. That's where I live on the reservation. Now it's your turn. Say something."

"Sorry," Jack wanted to apologize, but the word got stuck behind his teeth, his chattering teeth. Sleep reached out to him with icy arms. Did he hear far-away thunder? No, it was Indian drums. If his lips hadn't been so stiff with cold, he'd have smiled, because the warriors were coming to dance just for him.

The first warrior rode toward him on a tall horse. No, it wasn't a warrior, it was his father, Steven, on Hal. Jack wanted to run to him, but Steven vanished slowly into the mist.

"Bring him back," Jack tried to shout to Ethan, but when he opened his eyes, he knew why his father had disappeared. Ethan was making magic again. Raising the same cedar branch that had hurt Jack on the back of his head and smashed Steven's fingers, Ethan slapped it hard against the rock wall behind him. Again and again he smacked it, limb against rock, until the wood splintered and broke into pieces.

Now the real warriors came, their faces painted into frightening masks. All of them rode white horses, ghost horses, and all in a row they galloped toward Jack until they ran over the top of him, but they didn't hurt him. Their headdresses were made of feathers so bright they burned the backs of Jack's eyes. "Please bring back my father," he begged them. When he tried to get on his knees to beg, strong arms pushed him back down.

Then he smelled it. Cedar smoke. When he opened his eyes, the smoke stung them, but he could see that once more Ethan was working his magic. Ethan held flame in his fingers, flame that pushed against the green, wet foliage of the broken cedar branch. It didn't burn, even though Ethan blew on it; it just smoked into a cloud that covered Jack and hid the ghost horses. He knew that was supposed to happen—the smoke would hide them and they would disappear, only to reappear when the Shoshone danced the Ghost Dance.

Next came a lone Shoshone woman riding a sleek white mare that reared in front of Jack. He was afraid the horse's hoofs would crash down and break his skull just as the mustang had nearly crushed Ashley. Then his heart soared, because he knew this horse. It was Wild Spirit.

> *Stars paint Wild Spirit's track,*
> *They light a path through the velvet sky,*
> *And a woman rides her back.*

He could see stars painting a track through the velvet sky, but they were orange stars, sparks that flew up from the cedar branch Ethan waved as he muttered, "Can't get the stupid thing to burn."

And then a man and a woman came toward Jack. At first he thought the woman was Vivian Swallow, because she was dressed in white elkskin beaded with bright patterns, the kind Vivian had worn. But when she got close, Jack didn't recognize the woman or the man with her. He saw that their faces had no color. They were pale as—ghosts.

Jack tried to talk to them, but they reached out toward Ethan. He thought he heard them say, "Ethan," but then he realized that it was he, Jack, who was speaking the name.

"I'm right here," Ethan said. "But Jack, I gotta get you out of here. I can't get a fire started and you're breathing funny and your skin is as white as a ghost. We've been here over an hour. I think you're getting that—what do you call it—hypothermia."

I saw your mother and father, Jack wanted to tell him. They were here, trying to touch you.

"The water level is lower," Ethan was saying, "so I think—maybe—we can make it." Ethan looked worried. "Can you hear me, Jack?"

Jack's lips formed "yes."

"I'll blow up all these plastic bags like balloons and stick 'em in the backpacks. That'll make them like life preservers. It *might* work."

Jack drifted into his dreams again until he felt himself lifted roughly by Ethan.

"I'm trying to get this sweatshirt on you. Jeez, can't you help at all? Jack, I need you to wake up!"

Jack felt his left arm seized and jammed through the sleeve of the sweatshirt. Then his right arm. The jolt cleared his head a little.

"Open your eyes," Ethan ordered. "Look at me! I'm gonna jump into the water and then I'll pull you off this ledge, hear?

You gotta hang your arms around my neck so I can carry you. You gotta hold on."

"OK," Jack whispered around the throbbing inside his head.

He heard a splash. Then he felt himself dragged by the hands until he toppled over the edge of the rock ledge. The shock of water spluttering into his mouth sent him into a fit of coughing. "Why'd you do that?" he demanded of Ethan.

"Good! You're talking. Give me your hands, and don't fight me." Ethan slung Jack across his back, pulling Jack's wrists forward so that his arms draped across Ethan's shoulders. "Hang on."

One inflated backpack floated in front of Ethan, the other swung out behind Jack. Like the backpacks, Jack was floating, too, belly down, in the swollen Virgin River, his head leaning against Ethan's. This time his dreams were sweet and comforting. No more ghosts. Ethan's grunts and yells sometimes penetrated the dreams, as Ethan floundered, stepping into a hole or tripping on a submerged rock. Once Ethan jerked Jack's wrist forward and said, "Is your watch waterproof? If it's telling the right time, we've been slogging along like this for more than an hour. The current helps. It's pushing us forward."

"Are you swimming?" Jack asked drowsily.

"No, you jerk, I'm walking. How could I swim with you on my back? Anyway, I don't know how to swim."

"Really?" That surprising bit of information worked its way into Jack's consciousness. "Are you saving my life?" he asked next.

"Yeah, man, you got it," Ethan panted. "Like in the Ghost Dance, I'm bringing a dead person back to life."

CHAPTER ELEVEN

Up ahead!" Ethan cried. "I see people! Jack—we made it!"

"Cold," Jack mumbled.

"I know. So am I, and my back's killing me. Look, I need you to try to walk. The water's not so deep here, and you're heavy. Come on, move your legs. Right. Left. Right."

Rocks bumped against the sides of Jack's sneakers when Ethan stood him upright. As the canyon walls opened wider, the water level had gone down so that it was no more than waist deep. Placing as much weight on his feet as he could, Jack tried to stand, but his legs wouldn't hold him. They felt like two poles of ice that were no longer legs. His whole body had become stone. Ahead of him, he could see a kaleidoscope of colors in the distance, flashing lights that were as bright as red and blue suns.

"Hey! *Over here!*" Ethan shouted. He gave a loud, trilling Indian cry and waved an arm.

"Here," Jack whispered.

There was an eruption of what sounded like applause. Lifting his head, Jack saw dozens of people lined along the walkway that led to the mouth of The Narrows, people in yellow plastic ponchos and ranger uniforms. It was still hard for him to put sights and sounds together; it was as if images had been broken into pieces and scattered on the ground. But a voice—his mother's voice—pierced his consciousness.

"Jack! Jack! Are you all right?"

In his haze, Jack saw his mother's pale face, saw her arms reach for him, but two medics grabbed him first and began to carry him quickly to the riverbank. Another medic approached Ethan, but Jack could hear him say, "I made it all the way down. I can walk the rest of the way."

Water churned around Jack and then he saw rocks and the steps that led to the top of the trail. More people, more colors, more sounds fell on him like raindrops. "Mom?" he asked weakly.

"I'm right here. I'm right beside you," Olivia cried. Her voice sounded near and far at the same time, as if she were speaking inside a bubble. Was she crying? Jack tried to put the pieces together, but they came out all wrong, like a Picasso painting he'd seen in a book at school.

"Dad—where?"

He felt his mother's hand rest lightly against his cheek. "He's all right, Jack. He's in an ambulance."

"Ambulance?" Once again, nausea rose in Jack's throat in a wave that almost choked him.

"He's banged up, but he's OK. He broke some fingers. Jack—where do you hurt?"

"My head."

The two medics had him on a stretcher now, but they were moving too fast for Jack to see anything except a blur of tall cliffs and some unknown people's midriffs.

"You're going to have to step back, ma'am," he heard one of the medics say. "We've got to get an IV into him. Ned, his body temp's way too low. Get that heated blanket on him, and fast."

"Mom—" Jack croaked.

"I'm right here. Ashley's here, too. And Summer. Everything will be all right now. You're going to go to the hospital. You're safe."

"Ethan—" Jack swallowed, trying to get the words out. "He saved me."

His mother's face appeared in the sky over him. He couldn't really make it out except that her curly hair caught the sun like tiny shining spirals. "I know," he heard her say. "I know." And then Jack's lids drooped, and he drifted once more into darkness.

#

When he opened his eyes, he was in a pale green room with a tiny window that showed nothing but a square of blue sky. A clear tube snaked out of his wrist, and the sheets underneath him felt scratchy against his skin. Blinking, he slowly looked around. His mother dozed in an orange vinyl chair, her head bent to one side and her lips slightly parted. Beside her, with two fingers curved in metal splints, sat his dad, and to his right Jack saw Summer, Ashley, and Ethan hunched in three smaller chairs, watching what sounded like the Simpsons coming from a television hanging on a wall. He was in a hospital. Jack blinked again.

"Well, look who finally decided to join us," his father said.

His mother jolted upright. Leaning over, she kissed his forehead and smiled. Jack had never seen his mother look so old; dark half-moons smudged the skin beneath her eyes, and her face was as pale as a bleached sheet. The fine wrinkles around her mouth seemed deeper, as if worry had carved them. "Honey, how do you feel?" she asked softly. "How's your head?"

"My head?" Jack reached up and gingerly touched the back of his neck. He could still feel a dull throb. "It hurts. What happened?"

"What happened?" Ashley squeaked. She was on her feet, clamoring on the other side of Jack's bed. "You about scared us all to death. Mom and me and Summer were over at the Chloride Canyon 'cause Summer figured out what was wrong with the ghost horses. I mean, she told Mom and then Mom checked and sure enough, that was the reason."

"She did?" Jack began, but Ashley could not be stopped. A torrent of words as fast as the water in The Narrows spilled out of her mouth.

"And then one of the guys comes roaring up in his pickup and tells Mom that he heard there was a flash flood at Zion, and didn't she say that her family was hiking up there today? Man, you should have seen her, Jack. Mom drove about a hundred miles an hour. We must have made it from the Chloride Canyon to the park in ten minutes!"

"Ashley, I did not go a hundred miles an hour! Maybe it seemed that way—" Olivia blushed. "Well, yes, I was speeding, but no more than ten miles over the limit. Honest!"

"Uh-*huh.*" Ashley grinned. "And then Mom jumps out of the car and runs all the way up the trail, and Summer and I tried, but we couldn't keep up 'cause Mom kept running. When we finally caught up with her, Mom was trying to go into the river, but the rangers wouldn't let her because they said it was too dangerous, and it wouldn't help anybody if she drowned. And then later Dad came floating down, but you and Ethan were still gone, and—"

"Whoa, Ashley, slow down. Jack's had a concussion, you know," Steven told her, smiling. A dark bruise was beginning to form on Steven's brow right above his eye, and a gauze-and-adhesive bandage circled his forearm. He walked over and settled on the edge of the hospital bed, then with his good hand lightly touched the top of Jack's head.

"I'm so glad you're OK, Dad. When you got swept away…." Suddenly, Jack couldn't finish. Shadowy pictures of what had happened came and went through him, like a deck of cards with pictures being flipped behind his eyelids. Yet one image burned as if his mind had been branded, and that was of his father, arms flailing, snatched away by a wall of churning water. His dad could have died. They all could have.

"Hey, son, don't get upset. I'm fine. A bit banged up like you, but I'm here. Except—" Steven's face twisted into a mask of remorse. "Except that I feel so awful about what I did—taking you kids into so much danger. I should have checked the weather report at the back-country desk at the visitor center. I should have talked to the rangers before we left. But I thought, since we weren't going too far up the canyon—" Steven's voice choked. "I was wrong. And my negligence nearly cost us our lives."

Olivia put her arms around Steven and whispered, "They're safe now, sweetheart."

Ethan and Summer crowded the foot of Jack's bed, and, surprisingly, it was Ethan who broke the somber silence in the room. He grabbed Jack's toe and tweaked it, saying, "It's about time you woke up. You know what time it is? It's 11:00 in the morning. I've been sitting in that dumb chair for two hours already, but nobody feels sorry for me 'cause I don't have a lump on my head. If I had a lump, maybe I could be in one of these electronic beds and get my own television, too."

"Hey, Ethan," Jack said, grinning.

"Hey, yourself." Arching his spine, he told Jack, "Man, do you know how heavy you are? By the end I swear you must have weighed 300 pounds. And you kept talking about all kinds of crazy stuff, like you saw people dancing around and coming out of the rocks and shooting stars popping out of the water. You were out of it."

"You had hypothermia," Olivia interrupted. "Between that and the crack on your head, you were hallucinating. Jack, if it hadn't been for Ethan, the doctors think you wouldn't have made it. Your body temperature was dangerously low—any lower and your heart might have stopped altogether. Ethan got you out just in the nick of time. You owe him a lot. You owe him your life."

Jack looked at the foot of the bed and for the first time really saw Ethan. He'd never truly looked at him before, other than as an enemy he had to keep away from. Ethan had on an old striped cotton shirt and a pair of jeans that had been rubbed bare at the knees like any other kid's. With his hair hanging loose past his shoulders, he looked like an Indian. When he crossed his arms over his chest, he was a warrior. A real Shoshone brave—one who would save a friend. With a start, Jack realized that he was that friend.

"Thanks, Ethan," Jack said, his voice low.

"Hey, no big deal."

"Yes, it is."

Ethan just shrugged his shoulders, but a smile curled the edge of his lips like a tiny wave.

"Did I say a lot of stupid stuff?" Jack asked.

"Everything you said was stupid," Ethan answered, laughing.

"I don't know what happened. I kept seeing things. It was so weird—I saw people with their faces painted and this woman in a white dress."

"An angel?" Ashley asked.

"No—maybe. I don't know. Her dress was all beaded—it was like the kind we saw at Ethan's pow-wow, only this one had a long fringe at the edges that was like a foot long, and the woman had this white feather in her hair. And she kept going over to Ethan. And there was a man, too. He had on buckskin, and he had some kind of shield."

"Our mother had a white dress with fringe," Summer said softly. "After Mother died, Grandmother put the dress away. It's for me when I'm all grown up." Raising her eyes, she added, "And our mother wore a feather right here at the back of her head." She reached back to touch her crown. "Is that where you saw the feather?"

Jack began to nod, but stopped, because it hurt.

"And the shield the man carried, was it a wheel of blue feathers?"

Jack tried to remember. Was it blue? Or was his mind playing tricks on him again. "I—I think so," he stammered. "Maybe."

"Then the Ghost Dance worked, Ethan. Mother came back to you when you needed her. Father, too."

"They came for both of us," Ethan whispered. "For me and for Jack, too."

"You smelled the cedar smoke, didn't you?" Summer asked Jack.

A memory of smoke seemed to curl in his nostrils once again. "Yes."

Olivia bit the edge of her lip. "Kids, remember, Jack was hit on the head. And he also had hypothermia, which made him see things that weren't really there." Olivia rushed on before Summer could answer. "Things always have a logical explanation. Ethan, you said you tried to build a fire, right? Out of cedar? That's why Jack smelled smoke."

But Summer's dark eyes never left Jack's. "Did she say anything, Jack? Did my mother bring a message?"

"No. She tried to get to Ethan, though. The man kept reaching out his hands. I remember that much."

"They were there." Summer's dark eyes welled up with tears. With the palms of her hands she rubbed away the tears that spilled over. After that, nobody in the room seemed to know what to say, although Jack could tell that neither of his parents believed a word of it. Olivia looked at Steven, who nodded, moving his mouth as if he were carefully forming a reply that he didn't know whether he should make.

Suddenly the door to the room swung open, and a woman in pink scrubs with fuzzy blonde hair walked in carrying a tray of food. "Hello, everyone," she said in a cheery voice. "I see our patient is finally awake. Bet you're hungry, too. I've got just the thing for you, and if your family could all move back for just a second, I can set this tray down on your table." Orange juice with a tinfoil top, some bright yellow pudding, a banana, and green gelatin were crowded on the tray she pushed in front of Jack. When she picked up his wrist, pressing two fingers against his pulse, Jack noticed how cool her hand felt. Her lips barely moved as she counted the beats. A clipboard appeared, and after scribbling on the paper, she turned Jack's head so that she could examine the base of his skull.

"Looking real good. The doctor will be in soon, and then I think you're out of here, kiddo. Bet you're going to hate that, huh?"

"Nope," Jack said, opening his orange juice. When he took a sip, it felt cool and sweet in his mouth.

"If any of the rest of you would like some food, the cafeteria is on the first floor. You know, a year ago a couple of people got caught in The Narrows. They didn't make it out. You're a lucky young man," she said, clicking her pen shut. "You all were lucky."

The door closed behind her with a gentle puff of air, probably rigged, Jack guessed, to keep it from slamming and waking up other patients. What the nurse had said was true enough: Ethan, Jack, and his dad were lucky. Many people caught in a flash flood didn't live to tell about it. He would never forget how close they came to dying. Other people, like Ethan and Summer's parents, walked into death and never came out again. Had Ethan's mom and dad really visited Jack on that ledge? He tried to grab onto the memory, but it slipped through his mind like water, like smoke. Maybe they'd been there, or maybe he'd just dreamed it. He'd been raised to believe only what he could taste and touch; he couldn't make sense of seeing ghosts.

Ashley, who hated silences, broke the stillness that had settled on the room. "Jack, you didn't hear about the mustangs!" she exclaimed. "I was trying to tell you what Summer said to Mom. You know—how she solved the mystery!"

Summer? As quiet as a spirit, Summer returned Jack's gaze with her large, dark eyes.

"It was so amazing," Ashley bubbled on. "Before we knew there was a flood, we were talking to Art Meacham, you know, about the horses? They were penned in that water trap, and Mom went in, but she couldn't find one thing wrong with them. She looked all of them over from top to bottom, but she said they were healthy."

"That's right," Olivia agreed. "Everything seemed to check out just fine. The way they'd acted was a complete mystery. When that stallion almost ran over Ashley, I thought he must be demented. But when I examined him, I could tell he was perfectly normal. I couldn't figure out why he had run at Ashley like that."

"So then Summer said—tell Jack what you told Mom, Summer. Go on!" Ashley gave her a little shove toward the bed.

Summer's voice was as soft as wind chimes. "I said that these were ghost horses. I said that they were made to ride on the wind. I said they could see what others could not, and not see what others could."

"It was the word 'see' that stopped me cold," Olivia went on excitedly. "I'd checked everything—teeth, hoofs, muscles, tendons—but I hadn't once thought to really look into the mustangs' eyes. When I did, what do you think I discovered?"

"I don't know. What?" Jack asked.

"Cataracts. The white horses' lenses were so opaque from cataracts that they couldn't see at all. Those horses were completely blind!"

Ashley, who had pulled her hair into a high ponytail, nodded so hard it bounced against her back. "Only the white ones, though. The dark ones could see fine. It was as though they were talking real loud to the ghost horses so they would know what to do."

"Which was why the herd sounded so strange with all that extra whinnying," Olivia continued. "The amazing thing is the dark horses were actually leading the white horses around by sound and touch. Can you believe it? It was as if a sighted horse had been assigned by the herd to care for each handicapped white one. Art said he thought the white ones might have been sired by a domestic white stud that a rancher let loose on the range long ago. The story goes that the stud eventually went blind. Art thinks there's a genetic link to the blindness. For the most part, the horses can see when they're young, like Mariah, but after they're five or six years old, the cataracts develop." Shaking her head, Olivia said, "And we humans think we're so smart. Can you even imagine how hard it would be to survive in a place as harsh as that land and not be able to see at all? But I never would have caught on to it if it hadn't been for Summer."

"My sister sees what others don't," Ethan told them. "She has the gift of deep sight—like the ghost horses."

Steven shifted uncomfortably, but Ethan ignored him. "Early this morning, Summer and I talked. We have something to say." Summer, who was dressed again in the yellow sundress, hung back behind her brother, but Ethan stood tall, his arms crossed tightly. "We both wanted to say—we're sorry. For our dancing and for the bad things that happened. We don't want you

Landons to go away or disappear or leave us. Not anymore, anyway."

"Yes, well, there is absolutely no need to apologize," Steven assured the two of them.

"That's right, no apologies needed," Olivia echoed as Ashley chimed in her agreement.

"Whether you see it or not, there was magic. We won't use it again," Ethan promised.

In the pause, Steven cleared his throat. "Well, I'm sure Summer is very intuitive, and that's a wonderful gift, but you two didn't bring on any of those bad things. Stuff happens. Jack was wrong about some of it; I was very, very wrong, too, but no dance caused the flood or the rock slide or the mustang to nearly crash into Ashley. Only nature made those things happen." Steven rubbed the tips of his splints with his good hand. "OK?"

Jack nodded, understanding what his mother and father might not. There was seeing, and there was a larger kind of seeing. Before he was trapped in the flash flood, he thought Ethan was just a punky kid with insides as stony as his expression. Now, he knew Ethan was someone he could trust with his life. And maybe Ethan saw the Landons differently as well. Hadn't he just said he didn't want to leave them?

Jack looked at Ethan, at his stubbornness that now seemed strangely like pride, and at Summer, who seemed able to cross between this world and another one. Maybe it was true, maybe it wasn't, that there were different ways of seeing, but one thing Jack knew for sure: In Ethan, he saw a boy who would risk his own life to save Jack's. An Indian brave. No wonder they were called braves. Jack saw—in the boy who stood there in front of his bed, smiling at him—a true friend.

AFTERWORD

I grew up in the deep canyons and on the wide
ranges that inspired the thrilling tale you have just
read. The story, of course, is fiction, but the setting
is real. I can still feel the awe that engulfed me the
first time I looked up at those massive canyon walls.
We were on a family trip to my grandmother's
house—a journey that would take us through Zion
Canyon. By the time we got to Zion, I was fast asleep.
When Dad woke me, all I could see were gas
stations, motels, and souvenir shops. I wondered what
the big deal was. Then my father gently lifted my chin
with his fingers. As my eyes rose, I saw one of the
most glorious sights I have ever seen: Zion's towers
of stone lifting high into the heavens. Now, 40 years
later, I come to work in the canyon every day. From
my desk I can raise my chin, look up through my

office window at those massive canyon walls, and still feel the same wonder I felt as a boy.

Just as vivid is the memory of my first look at wild mustangs. My father was a rancher, so I spent a lot of days riding horseback with him. One day we were riding through a thick stand of juniper trees in search of cattle when suddenly we broke into a clearing. There, little more than a hundred yards away, was a band of wild horses grazing. The wind was in our faces so the mustangs weren't aware of our approach. It was an amazing sight. My heart boomed in my chest like a kettle drum. Dad and I sat on our horses at the edge of the clearing for a long time, whispering our thoughts back and forth to each other while we watched them graze. To my dad the mustangs were mostly a nuisance, because they competed for the same precious grass that sustained our cows. I was surprised that the mustangs looked small and mangy—not large and regal as I had expected. It wasn't until they caught sight of us and whirled away in a thunderball of dust that they took on a much more majestic appearance. Pounding out across the open sage with their heads high and their tails raised, they took on that noble look I had always imagined mustangs would have.

In that short encounter I learned something I have never forgotten: Things are not always what we imagine them to be. That day I began to understand that different people look at our public lands in different ways. Some people see them as wide-open spaces of wonder; others see them as great repositories of natural resources, like grass for cattle, minerals for mining, and trees for lumber.

The state of Utah, where most of this story takes place, consists of nearly 85,000 square miles of land. Believe it or not, you could fit Maine, Vermont, New Hampshire, Connecticut, New Jersey, Massachusetts, and Maryland inside the borders of Utah and almost have room for Rhode Island. What is most amazing, though, is that 67 percent of Utah is public land. That means it is owned and managed by the federal government, which, in turn, means it is owned and managed by the citizens of the United States—you and me. Indeed, about two-thirds of all the land in the United States is owned by the federal government.

This book introduces you to two different kinds of public lands—the lands administered by the National Park Service (NPS) and the lands administered by the Bureau of Land Management (BLM). Each of these agencies has a different mission. The mission of the National Park Service is to "preserve unimpaired the natural and cultural resources and values of the National Park System for the enjoyment, education, and inspiration of this and future generations." The Bureau of Land Management has a "multiple-use" mandate to "manage the public land

and its vast array of resources in a way that benefits both present and future generations." Because they have different missions, these two federal agencies manage the lands under their jurisdictions in very different ways. The National Park Service approach to an issue will likely be different from the approach taken by the Bureau of Land Management.

When Jack, Ashley, Ethan, and Summer are in Zion National Park, they are in a place that is being preserved unimpaired. But when they are on the Chloride range with the wild horses, they are on land that is managed for many uses, including rangeland for wild horses and cattle. A ranger in Zion National Park, for example, is concerned about preserving things as they are. A BLM range manager on the Chloride range is concerned about maintaining a healthy habitat where wild horses and domestic cattle can prosper. It is amazing that the blind wild mustangs have managed to survive. But the future health of the herd may require BLM management to introduce other stallions and mares into the area to change the genetics of the herd.

It is important to understand the different uses of our public lands. Remember, these lands belong to you and me. In order for us to continue to prosper as a nation, we must wisely use the natural resources found on some of these lands. But special places like Zion National Park will continue to be protected "unimpaired" so that generations from now a father still can lift his child's chin and point his or her eyes upward toward sights that fill the soul with awe and wonder and joy.

Lyman Hafen
Executive Director
Zion Natural History Association

DON'T MISS—

WOLF STALKER
MYSTERY #1
Fast-paced adventure has the Landons on the trail of an injured wolf in Yellowstone National Park.

CLIFF-HANGER
MYSTERY #2
Jack's desire to help the headstrong Lucky Deal brings him face-to-face with a hungry cougar in Mesa Verde National Park.

DEADLY WATERS
MYSTERY #3
Jack and Ashley's efforts to save an injured manatee involve them in a thrilling chase through the Everglades.

RAGE OF FIRE
MYSTERY #4
In this tale of myth and mystery, a Vietnamese orphan named Danny leads Ashley and Jack into a steaming volcano in Hawaii Volcanoes National Park.

THE HUNTED
MYSTERY #5
While attempting to help a young Mexican runaway, Jack and Ashley flee for their lives from an enraged mother grizzly in Glacier National Park.

COMING SOON—

OVER THE EDGE
MYSTERY #7

ABOUT THE AUTHORS

An award-winning mystery writer and an award-winning science writer—who are also mother and daughter—are working together on Mysteries in Our National Parks!

Alane (Lanie) Ferguson's first mystery, *Show Me the Evidence,* won the Edgar Award, given by the Mystery Writers of America.

Gloria Skurzynski's *Almost the Real Thing* won the American Institute of Physics Science Writing Award.

Lanie lives in Elizabeth, Colorado. Gloria lives in Salt Lake City, Utah. To work together on a novel, they connect by phone, fax, and e-mail and "often forget which one of us wrote a particular line."

Gloria's e-mail: gloriabooks@qwest.net
Her Web site: http://gloriabooks.com
Lanie's e-mail: aferguson@sprynet.com